The Rights
and Wrongs
of Abortion

The Rights and Wrongs of Abortion

A *Philosophy & Public Affairs* Reader

Edited by MARSHALL COHEN, THOMAS NAGEL, and THOMAS SCANLON

Contributors

JOHN FINNIS

JUDITH JARVIS THOMSON

MICHAEL TOOLEY

ROGER WERTHEIMER

Princeton University Press
Princeton, New Jersey

The essays in this book originally appeared
in the quarterly journal *Philosophy &
Public Affairs*, published by Princeton
University Press.

Judith Jarvis Thomson, "A Defense of
Abortion," *P&PA* 1, no. 1 (Fall 1971);
Roger Wertheimer, "Understanding the
Abortion Argument," *P&PA* 1, no. 1 (Fall
1971): copyright © 1971 by Princeton
University Press. Michael Tooley,
"Abortion and Infanticide," *P&PA* 2, no. 1
(Fall 1972): copyright © 1972 by
Princeton University Press. John Finnis,
"The Rights and Wrongs of Abortion,"
P&PA 2, no. 2 (Winter 1973); Judith
Jarvis Thomson, "Rights and Deaths,"
P&PA 2, no. 2 (Winter 1973): copyright
© 1973 by Princeton University Press.
Michael Tooley, "A Postscript":
copyright © 1974 by Princeton University
Press.

First Princeton Paperback Printing, 1974
First Hardcover Printing, 1974

Printed in the United States of America by
Princeton University Press
Princeton, New Jersey

CONTENTS

PREFACE

Philosophy & Public Affairs was founded in the belief that issues of public concern often have an important philosophical dimension and that a philosophical examination of these issues can contribute to their clarification and to their resolution. The editors believe that this expectation is borne out by the following essays, drawn from the first two volumes of *Philosophy & Public Affairs*. The essays are reprinted here in the order of their appearance in the journal (with a postscript added in one case). They form a consecutive discussion of such fundamental issues as whether a woman has a right to decide what happens in and to her body; whether the fetus is a person; whether it has a right to life; whether there is, in fact, a morally significant difference between abortion and infanticide. These essays are part of an ongoing discussion which can be expected to continue. But they have permanently altered the character of the debate, introducing greater rigor and opening up entirely new questions. They constitute an indispensable source for anyone wishing to think further about the problem of abortion.

M.C., T.N., T.S.

The Rights
and Wrongs
of Abortion

JUDITH JARVIS THOMSON   A Defense of Abortion[1]

Most opposition to abortion relies on the premise that the fetus is a
human being, a person, from the moment of conception. The premise
is argued for, but, as I think, not well. Take, for example, the most
common argument. We are asked to notice that the development of
a human being from conception through birth into childhood is continuous; then it is said that to draw a line, to choose a point in this
development and say "before this point the thing is not a person, after
this point it is a person" is to make an arbitrary choice, a choice for
which in the nature of things no good reason can be given. It is concluded that the fetus is, or anyway that we had better say it is, a person from the moment of conception. But this conclusion does not follow. Similar things might be said about the development of an acorn
into an oak tree, and it does not follow that acorns are oak trees, or
that we had better say they are. Arguments of this form are sometimes
called "slippery slope arguments"—the phrase is perhaps self-explana-
tory—and it is dismaying that opponents of abortion rely on them so
heavily and uncritically.

I am inclined to agree, however, that the prospects for "drawing a
line" in the development of the fetus look dim. I am inclined to think
also that we shall probably have to agree that the fetus has already
become a human person well before birth. Indeed, it comes as a surprise when one first learns how early in its life it begins to acquire
human characteristics. By the tenth week, for example, it already has

1. I am very much indebted to James Thomson for discussion, criticism, and
many helpful suggestions.

a face, arms and legs, fingers and toes; it has internal organs, and brain activity is detectable.[2] On the other hand, I think that the premise is false, that the fetus is not a person from the moment of conception. A newly fertilized ovum, a newly implanted clump of cells, is no more a person than an acorn is an oak tree. But I shall not discuss any of this. For it seems to me to be of great interest to ask what happens if, for the sake of argument, we allow the premise. How, precisely, are we supposed to get from there to the conclusion that abortion is morally impermissible? Opponents of abortion commonly spend most of their time establishing that the fetus is a person, and hardly any time explaining the step from there to the impermissibility of abortion. Perhaps they think the step too simple and obvious to require much comment. Or perhaps instead they are simply being economical in argument. Many of those who defend abortion rely on the premise that the fetus is not a person, but only a bit of tissue that will become a person at birth; and why pay out more arguments than you have to? Whatever the explanation, I suggest that the step they take is neither easy nor obvious, that it calls for closer examination than it is commonly given, and that when we do give it this closer examination we shall feel inclined to reject it.

I propose, then, that we grant that the fetus is a person from the moment of conception. How does the argument go from here? Something like this, I take it. Every person has a right to life. So the fetus has a right to life. No doubt the mother has a right to decide what shall happen in and to her body; everyone would grant that. But surely a person's right to life is stronger and more stringent than the mother's right to decide what happens in and to her body, and so outweighs it. So the fetus may not be killed; an abortion may not be performed.

It sounds plausible. But now let me ask you to imagine this. You wake up in the morning and find yourself back to back in bed with an unconscious violinist. A famous unconscious violinist. He has been found to have a fatal kidney ailment, and the Society of Music Lovers

2. Daniel Callahan, *Abortion: Law, Choice and Morality* (New York, 1970), p. 373. This book gives a fascinating survey of the available information on abortion. The Jewish tradition is surveyed in David M. Feldman, *Birth Control in Jewish Law* (New York, 1968), Part 5, the Catholic tradition in John T. Noonan, Jr., "An Almost Absolute Value in History," in *The Morality of Abortion*, ed. John T. Noonan, Jr. (Cambridge, Mass., 1970).

has canvassed all the available medical records and found that you alone have the right blood type to help. They have therefore kidnapped you, and last night the violinist's circulatory system was plugged into yours, so that your kidneys can be used to extract poisons from his blood as well as your own. The director of the hospital now tells you, "Look, we're sorry the Society of Music Lovers did this to you—we would never have permitted it if we had known. But still, they did it, and the violinist now is plugged into you. To unplug you would be to kill him. But never mind, it's only for nine months. By then he will have recovered from his ailment, and can safely be unplugged from you." Is it morally incumbent on you to accede to this situation? No doubt it would be very nice of you if you did, a great kindness. But do you *have* to accede to it? What if it were not nine months, but nine years? Or longer still? What if the director of the hospital says, "Tough luck, I agree, but you've now got to stay in bed, with the violinist plugged into you, for the rest of your life. Because remember this. All persons have a right to life, and violinists are persons. Granted you have a right to decide what happens in and to your body, but a person's right to life outweighs your right to decide what happens in and to your body. So you cannot ever be unplugged from him." I imagine you would regard this as outrageous, which suggests that something really is wrong with that plausible-sounding argument I mentioned a moment ago.

In this case, of course, you were kidnapped; you didn't volunteer for the operation that plugged the violinist into your kidneys. Can those who oppose abortion on the ground I mentioned make an exception for a pregnancy due to rape? Certainly. They can say that persons have a right to life only if they didn't come into existence because of rape; or they can say that all persons have a right to life, but that some have less of a right to life than others, in particular, that those who came into existence because of rape have less. But these statements have a rather unpleasant sound. Surely the question of whether you have a right to life at all, or how much of it you have, shouldn't turn on the question of whether or not you are the product of a rape. And in fact the people who oppose abortion on the ground I mentioned do not make this distinction, and hence do not make an exception in case of rape.

Nor do they make an exception for a case in which the mother has to spend the nine months of her pregnancy in bed. They would agree that would be a great pity, and hard on the mother; but all the same, all persons have a right to life, the fetus is a person, and so on. I suspect, in fact, that they would not make an exception for a case in which, miraculously enough, the pregnancy went on for nine years, or even the rest of the mother's life.

Some won't even make an exception for a case in which continuation of the pregnancy is likely to shorten the mother's life; they regard abortion as impermissible even to save the mother's life. Such cases are nowadays very rare, and many opponents of abortion do not accept this extreme view. All the same, it is a good place to begin: a number of points of interest come out in respect to it.

_1._ Let us call the view that abortion is impermissible even to save the mother's life "the extreme view." I want to suggest first that it does not issue from the argument I mentioned earlier without the addition of some fairly powerful premises. Suppose a woman has become pregnant, and now learns that she has a cardiac condition such that she will die if she carries the baby to term. What may be done for her? The fetus, being a person, has a right to life, but as the mother is a person too, so has she a right to life. Presumably they have an equal right to life. How is it supposed to come out that an abortion may not be performed? If mother and child have an equal right to life, shouldn't we perhaps flip a coin? Or should we add to the mother's right to life her right to decide what happens in and to her body, which everybody seems to be ready to grant—the sum of her rights now outweighing the fetus' right to life?

The most familiar argument here is the following. We are told that performing the abortion would be directly killing[3] the child, whereas doing nothing would not be killing the mother, but only letting her die. Moreover, in killing the child, one would be killing an innocent person, for the child has committed no crime, and is not aiming at his mother's death. And then there are a variety of ways in which this

3. The term "direct" in the arguments I refer to is a technical one. Roughly, what is meant by "direct killing" is either killing as an end in itself, or killing as a means to some end, for example, the end of saving someone else's life. See note 6, below, for an example of its use.

might be continued. (1) But as directly killing an innocent person is always and absolutely impermissible, an abortion may not be performed. Or, (2) as directly killing an innocent person is murder, and murder is always and absolutely impermissible, an abortion may not be performed.[4] Or, (3) as one's duty to refrain from directly killing an innocent person is more stringent than one's duty to keep a person from dying, an abortion may not be performed. Or, (4) if one's only options are directly killing an innocent person or letting a person die, one must prefer letting the person die, and thus an abortion may not be performed.[5]

Some people seem to have thought that these are not further premises which must be added if the conclusion is to be reached, but that they follow from the very fact that an innocent person has a right to life.[6] But this seems to me to be a mistake, and perhaps the simplest way to show this is to bring out that while we must certainly grant that innocent persons have a right to life, the theses in (1) through (4) are all false. Take (2), for example. If directly killing an innocent person is murder, and thus is impermissible, then the mother's directly killing the innocent person inside her is murder, and thus is

4. Cf. *Encyclical Letter of Pope Pius XI on Christian Marriage*, St. Paul Editions (Boston, n.d.), p. 32: "however much we may pity the mother whose health and even life is gravely imperiled in the performance of the duty allotted to her by nature, nevertheless what could ever be a sufficient reason for excusing in any way the direct murder of the innocent? This is precisely what we are dealing with here." Noonan (*The Morality of Abortion*, p. 43) reads this as follows: "What cause can ever avail to excuse in any way the direct killing of the innocent? For it is a question of that."

5. The thesis in (4) is in an interesting way weaker than those in (1), (2), and (3): they rule out abortion even in cases in which both mother *and* child will die if the abortion is not performed. By contrast, one who held the view expressed in (4) could consistently say that one needn't prefer letting two persons die to killing one.

6. Cf. the following passage from Pius XII, *Address to the Italian Catholic Society of Midwives*: "The baby in the maternal breast has the right to life immediately from God.—Hence there is no man, no human authority, no science, no medical, eugenic, social, economic or moral 'indication' which can establish or grant a valid juridical ground for a direct deliberate disposition of an innocent human life, that is a disposition which looks to its destruction either as an end or as a means to another end perhaps in itself not illicit.—The baby, still not born, is a man in the same degree and for the same reason as the mother" (quoted in Noonan, *The Morality of Abortion*, p. 45).

impermissible. But it cannot seriously be thought to be murder if the mother performs an abortion on herself to save her life. It cannot seriously be said that she *must* refrain, that she *must* sit passively by and wait for her death. Let us look again at the case of you and the violinist. There you are, in bed with the violinist, and the director of the hospital says to you, "It's all most distressing, and I deeply sympathize, but you see this is putting an additional strain on your kidneys, and you'll be dead within the month. But you *have* to stay where you are all the same. Because unplugging you would be directly killing an innocent violinist, and that's murder, and that's impermissible." If anything in the world is true, it is that you do not commit murder, you do not do what is impermissible, if you reach around to your back and unplug yourself from that violinist to save your life.

The main focus of attention in writings on abortion has been on what a third party may or may not do in answer to a request from a woman for an abortion. This is in a way understandable. Things being as they are, there isn't much a woman can safely do to abort herself. So the question asked is what a third party may do, and what the mother may do, if it is mentioned at all, is deduced, almost as an afterthought, from what it is concluded that third parties may do. But it seems to me that to treat the matter in this way is to refuse to grant to the mother that very status of person which is so firmly insisted on for the fetus. For we cannot simply read off what a person may do from what a third party may do. Suppose you find yourself trapped in a tiny house with a growing child. I mean a very tiny house, and a rapidly growing child—you are already up against the wall of the house and in a few minutes you'll be crushed to death. The child on the other hand won't be crushed to death; if nothing is done to stop him from growing he'll be hurt, but in the end he'll simply burst open the house and walk out a free man. Now I could well understand it if a bystander were to say, "There's nothing we can do for you. We cannot choose between your life and his, we cannot be the ones to decide who is to live, we cannot intervene." But it cannot be concluded that you too can do nothing, that you cannot attack it to save your life. However innocent the child may be, you do not have to wait passively while it crushes you to death. Perhaps a pregnant woman is vaguely felt to have the status of house, to which we don't allow the right of self-defense. But if the woman houses the child, it should be remembered that she is a person who houses it.

I should perhaps stop to say explicitly that I am not claiming that people have a right to do anything whatever to save their lives. I think, rather, that there are drastic limits to the right of self-defense. If someone threatens you with death unless you torture someone else to death, I think you have not the right, even to save your life, to do so. But the case under consideration here is very different. In our case there are only two people involved, one whose life is threatened, and one who threatens it. Both are innocent: the one who is threatened is not threatened because of any fault, the one who threatens does not threaten because of any fault. For this reason we may feel that we bystanders cannot intervene. But the person threatened can.

In sum, a woman surely can defend her life against the threat to it posed by the unborn child, even if doing so involves its death. And this shows not merely that the theses in (1) through (4) are false; it shows also that the extreme view of abortion is false, and so we need not canvass any other possible ways of arriving at it from the argument I mentioned at the outset.

2. The extreme view could of course be weakened to say that while abortion is permissible to save the mother's life, it may not be performed by a third party, but only by the mother herself. But this cannot be right either. For what we have to keep in mind is that the mother and the unborn child are not like two tenants in a small house which has, by an unfortunate mistake, been rented to both: the mother *owns* the house. The fact that she does adds to the offensiveness of deducing that the mother can do nothing from the supposition that third parties can do nothing. But it does more than this: it casts a bright light on the supposition that third parties can do nothing. Certainly it lets us see that a third party who says "I cannot choose between you" is fooling himself if he thinks this is impartiality. If Jones has found and fastened on a certain coat, which he needs to keep him from freezing, but which Smith also needs to keep him from freezing, then it is not impartiality that says "I cannot choose between you" when Smith owns the coat. Women have said again and again "This body is *my* body!" and they have reason to feel angry, reason to feel that it has been like shouting into the wind. Smith, after all, is

hardly likely to bless us if we say to him, "Of course it's your coat, anybody would grant that it is. But no one may choose between you and Jones who is to have it."

We should really ask what it is that says "no one may choose" in the face of the fact that the body that houses the child is the mother's body. It may be simply a failure to appreciate this fact. But it may be something more interesting, namely the sense that one has a right to refuse to lay hands on people, even where it would be just and fair to do so, even where justice seems to require that somebody do so. Thus justice might call for somebody to get Smith's coat back from Jones, and yet you have a right to refuse to be the one to lay hands on Jones, a right to refuse to do physical violence to him. This, I think, must be granted. But then what should be said is not "no one may choose," but only "*I* cannot choose," and indeed not even this, but "*I* will not *act*," leaving it open that somebody else can or should, and in particular that anyone in a position of authority, with the job of securing people's rights, both can and should. So this is no difficulty. I have not been arguing that any given third party must accede to the mother's request that he perform an abortion to save her life, but only that he may.

I suppose that in some views of human life the mother's body is only on loan to her, the loan not being one which gives her any prior claim to it. One who held this view might well think it impartiality to say "I cannot choose." But I shall simply ignore this possibility. My own view is that if a human being has any just, prior claim to anything at all, he has a just, prior claim to his own body. And perhaps this needn't be argued for here anyway, since, as I mentioned, the arguments against abortion we are looking at do grant that the woman has a right to decide what happens in and to her body.

But although they do grant it, I have tried to show that they do not take seriously what is done in granting it. I suggest the same thing will reappear even more clearly when we turn away from cases in which the mother's life is at stake, and attend, as I propose we now do, to the vastly more common cases in which a woman wants an abortion for some less weighty reason than preserving her own life.

3. Where the mother's life is not at stake, the argument I mentioned at the outset seems to have a much stronger pull. "Everyone

has a right to life, so the unborn person has a right to life." And isn't the child's right to life weightier than anything other than the mother's own right to life, which she might put forward as ground for an abortion?

This argument treats the right to life as if it were unproblematic. It is not, and this seems to me to be precisely the source of the mistake.

For we should now, at long last, ask what it comes to, to have a right to life. In some views having a right to life includes having a right to be given at least the bare minimum one needs for continued life. But suppose that what in fact *is* the bare minimum a man needs for continued life is something he has no right at all to be given? If I am sick unto death, and the only thing that will save my life is the touch of Henry Fonda's cool hand on my fevered brow, then all the same, I have no right to be given the touch of Henry Fonda's cool hand on my fevered brow. It would be frightfully nice of him to fly in from the West Coast to provide it. It would be less nice, though no doubt well meant, if my friends flew out to the West Coast and carried Henry Fonda back with them. But I have no right at all against anybody that he should do this for me. Or again, to return to the story I told earlier, the fact that for continued life that violinist needs the continued use of your kidneys does not establish that he has a right to be given the continued use of your kidneys. He certainly has no right against you that *you* should give him continued use of your kidneys. For nobody has any right to use your kidneys unless you give him such a right; and nobody has the right against you that you shall give him this right—if you do allow him to go on using your kidneys, this is a kindness on your part, and not something he can claim from you as his due. Nor has he any right against anybody else that *they* should give him continued use of your kidneys. Certainly he had no right against the Society of Music Lovers that they should plug him into you in the first place. And if you now start to unplug yourself, having learned that you will otherwise have to spend nine years in bed with him, there is nobody in the world who must try to prevent you, in order to see to it that he is given something he has a right to be given.

Some people are rather stricter about the right to life. In their view, it does not include the right to be given anything, but amounts to, and only to, the right not to be killed by anybody. But here a related difficulty arises. If everybody is to refrain from killing that violinist, then everybody must refrain from doing a great many different sorts of things. Everybody must refrain from slitting his throat, everybody must refrain from shooting him—and everybody must refrain from unplugging you from him. But does he have a right against everybody that they shall refrain from unplugging you from him? To refrain from doing this is to allow him to continue to use your kidneys. It could be argued that he has a right against us that *we* should allow him to continue to use your kidneys. That is, while he had no right against us that we should give him the use of your kidneys, it might be argued that he anyway has a right against us that we shall not now intervene and deprive him of the use of your kidneys. I shall come back to third-party interventions later. But certainly the violinist has no right against you that *you* shall allow him to continue to use your kidneys. As I said, if you do allow him to use them, it is a kindness on your part, and not something you owe him.

The difficulty I point to here is not peculiar to the right to life. It reappears in connection with all the other natural rights; and it is something which an adequate account of rights must deal with. For present purposes it is enough just to draw attention to it. But I would stress that I am not arguing that people do not have a right to life— quite to the contrary, it seems to me that the primary control we must place on the acceptability of an account of rights is that it should turn out in that account to be a truth that all persons have a right to life. I am arguing only that having a right to life does not guarantee having either a right to be given the use of or a right to be allowed continued use of another person's body—even if one needs it for life itself. So the right to life will not serve the opponents of abortion in the very simple and clear way in which they seem to have thought it would.

4. There is another way to bring out the difficulty. In the most ordinary sort of case, to deprive someone of what he has a right to is to treat him unjustly. Suppose a boy and his small brother are jointly given a box of chocolates for Christmas. If the older boy takes the box and refuses to give his brother any of the chocolates, he is unjust to him, for the brother has been given a right to half of them. But

suppose that, having learned that otherwise it means nine years in
bed with that violinist, you unplug yourself from him. You surely are
not being unjust to him, for you gave him no right to use your kidneys, and no one else can have given him any such right. But we have
to notice that in unplugging yourself, you are killing him; and violinists, like everybody else, have a right to life, and thus in the view we
were considering just now, the right not to be killed. So here you do
what he supposedly has a right you shall not do, but you do not act
unjustly to him in doing it.

The emendation which may be made at this point is this: the right √
to life consists not in the right not to be killed, but rather in the right
not to be killed unjustly. This runs a risk of circularity, but never
mind: it would enable us to square the fact that the violinist has a
right to life with the fact that you do not act unjustly toward him in
unplugging yourself, thereby killing him. For if you do not kill him
unjustly, you do not violate his right to life, and so it is no wonder
you do him no injustice.

But if this emendation is accepted, the gap in the argument against
abortion stares us plainly in the face: it is by no means enough to
show that the fetus is a person, and to remind us that all persons have
a right to life—we need to be shown also that killing the fetus violates
its right to life, i.e., that abortion is unjust killing. And is it?

I suppose we may take it as a datum that in a case of pregnancy
due to rape the mother has not given the unborn person a right to the
use of her body for food and shelter. Indeed, in what pregnancy could
it be supposed that the mother has given the unborn person such a
right? It is not as if there were unborn persons drifting about the
world, to whom a woman who wants a child says "I invite you in."

But it might be argued that there are other ways one can have
acquired a right to the use of another person's body than by having
been invited to use it by that person. Suppose a woman voluntarily
indulges in intercourse, knowing of the chance it will issue in pregnancy, and then she does become pregnant; is she not in part responsible for the presence, in fact the very existence, of the unborn person
inside her? No doubt she did not invite it in. But doesn't her partial
responsibility for its being there itself give it a right to the use of her

body?[7] If so, then her aborting it would be more like the boy's taking away the chocolates, and less like your unplugging yourself from the violinist—doing so would be depriving it of what it does have a right to, and thus would be doing it an injustice.

And then, too, it might be asked whether or not she can kill it even to save her own life: If she voluntarily called it into existence, how can she now kill it, even in self-defense?

The first thing to be said about this is that it is something new. Opponents of abortion have been so concerned to make out the independence of the fetus, in order to establish that it has a right to life, just as its mother does, that they have tended to overlook the possible support they might gain from making out that the fetus is *dependent* on the mother, in order to establish that she has a special kind of responsibility for it, a responsibility that gives it rights against her which are not possessed by any independent person—such as an ailing violinist who is a stranger to her.

On the other hand, this argument would give the unborn person a right to its mother's body only if her pregnancy resulted from a voluntary act, undertaken in full knowledge of the chance a pregnancy might result from it. It would leave out entirely the unborn person whose existence is due to rape. Pending the availability of some further argument, then, we would be left with the conclusion that unborn persons whose existence is due to rape have no right to the use of their mothers' bodies, and thus that aborting them is not depriving them of anything they have a right to and hence is not unjust killing.

And we should also notice that it is not at all plain that this argument really does go even as far as it purports to. For there are cases and cases, and the details make a difference. If the room is stuffy, and I therefore open a window to air it, and a burglar climbs in, it would be absurd to say,"Ah, now he can stay, she's given him a right to the use of her house—for she is partially responsible for his presence there, having voluntarily done what enabled him to get in, in full knowledge that there are such things as burglars, and that burglars

7. The need for a discussion of this argument was brought home to me by members of the Society for Ethical and Legal Philosophy, to whom this paper was originally presented.

burgle." It would be still more absurd to say this if I had had bars installed outside my windows, precisely to prevent burglars from getting in, and a burglar got in only because of a defect in the bars. It remains equally absurd if we imagine it is not a burglar who climbs in, but an innocent person who blunders or falls in. Again, suppose it were like this: people-seeds drift about in the air like pollen, and if you open your windows, one may drift in and take root in your carpets or upholstery. You don't want children, so you fix up your windows with fine mesh screens, the very best you can buy. As can happen, however, and on very, very rare occasions does happen, one of the screens is defective; and a seed drifts in and takes root. Does the person-plant who now develops have a right to the use of your house? Surely not—despite the fact that you voluntarily opened your windows, you knowingly kept carpets and upholstered furniture, and you knew that screens were sometimes defective. Someone may argue that you are responsible for its rooting, that it does have a right to your house, because after all you *could* have lived out your life with bare floors and furniture, or with sealed windows and doors. But this won't do—for by the same token anyone can avoid a pregnancy due to rape by having a hysterectomy, or anyway by never leaving home without a (reliable!) army.

It seems to me that the argument we are looking at can establish at most that there are *some* cases in which the unborn person has a right to the use of its mother's body, and therefore *some* cases in which abortion is unjust killing. There is room for much discussion and argument as to precisely which, if any. But I think we should sidestep this issue and leave it open, for at any rate the argument certainly does not establish that all abortion is unjust killing.

5. There is room for yet another argument here, however. We surely must all grant that there may be cases in which it would be morally indecent to detach a person from your body at the cost of his life. Suppose you learn that what the violinist needs is not nine years of your life, but only one hour: all you need do to save his life is to spend one hour in that bed with him. Suppose also that letting him use your kidneys for that one hour would not affect your health in the slightest. Admittedly you were kidnapped. Admittedly you did not give

anyone permission to plug him into you. Nevertheless it seems to me plain you *ought* to allow him to use your kidneys for that hour—it would be indecent to refuse.

Again, suppose pregnancy lasted only an hour, and constituted no threat to life or health. And suppose that a woman becomes pregnant as a result of rape. Admittedly she did not voluntarily do anything to bring about the existence of a child. Admittedly she did nothing at all which would give the unborn person a right to the use of her body. All the same it might well be said, as in the newly emended violinist story, that she *ought* to allow it to remain for that hour—that it would be indecent in her to refuse.

Now some people are inclined to use the term "right" in such a way that it follows from the fact that you ought to allow a person to use your body for the hour he needs, that he has a right to use your body for the hour he needs, even though he has not been given that right by any person or act. They may say that it follows also that if you refuse, you act unjustly toward him. This use of the term is perhaps so common that it cannot be called wrong; nevertheless it seems to me to be an unfortunate loosening of what we would do better to keep a tight rein on. Suppose that box of chocolates I mentioned earlier had not been given to both boys jointly, but was given only to the older boy. There he sits, stolidly eating his way through the box, his small brother watching enviously. Here we are likely to say "You ought not to be so mean. You ought to give your brother some of those chocolates." My own view is that it just does not follow from the truth of this that the brother has any right to any of the chocolates. If the boy refuses to give his brother any, he is greedy, stingy, callous—but not unjust. I suppose that the people I have in mind will say it does follow that the brother has a right to some of the chocolates, and thus that the boy does act unjustly if he refuses to give his brother any. But the effect of saying this is to obscure what we should keep distinct, namely the difference between the boy's refusal in this case and the boy's refusal in the earlier case, in which the box was given to both boys jointly, and in which the small brother thus had what was from any point of view clear title to half.

A further objection to so using the term "right" that from the fact that A ought to do a thing for B, it follows that B has a right against A that A do it for him, is that it is going to make the question of whether or not a man has a right to a thing turn on how easy it is to provide him with it; and this seems not merely unfortunate, but morally unacceptable. Take the case of Henry Fonda again. I said earlier that I had no right to the touch of his cool hand on my fevered brow, even though I needed it to save my life. I said it would be frightfully nice of him to fly in from the West Coast to provide me with it, but that I had no right against him that he should do so. But suppose he isn't on the West Coast. Suppose he has only to walk across the room, place a hand briefly on my brow—and lo, my life is saved. Then surely he ought to do it, it would be indecent to refuse. Is it to be said "Ah, well, it follows that in this case she has a right to the touch of his hand on her brow, and so it would be an injustice in him to refuse"? So that I have a right to it when it is easy for him to provide it, though no right when it's hard? It's rather a shocking idea that anyone's rights should fade away and disappear as it gets harder and harder to accord them to him.

So my own view is that even though you ought to let the violinist use your kidneys for the one hour he needs, we should not conclude that he has a right to do so—we should say that if you refuse, you are, like the boy who owns all the chocolates and will give none away, self-centered and callous, indecent in fact, but not unjust. And similarly, that even supposing a case in which a woman pregnant due to rape ought to allow the unborn person to use her body for the hour he needs, we should not conclude that he has a right to do so; we should conclude that she is self-centered, callous, indecent, but not unjust, if she refuses. The complaints are no less grave; they are just different. However, there is no need to insist on this point. If anyone does wish to deduce "he has a right" from "you ought," then all the same he must surely grant that there are cases in which it is not morally required of you that you allow that violinist to use your kidneys, and in which he does not have a right to use them, and in which you do not do him an injustice if you refuse. And so also for mother and unborn child. Except in such cases as the unborn person has a right to demand it—and we were leaving open the possibility that there may be such cases—nobody is morally *required* to make large sacrifices, of health, of all other interests and concerns, of all other duties

and commitments, for nine years, or even for nine months, in order
to keep another person alive.

6. We have in fact to distinguish between two kinds of Samaritan:
the Good Samaritan and what we might call the Minimally Decent
Samaritan. The story of the Good Samaritan, you will remember, goes
like this:

> A certain man went down from Jerusalem to Jericho, and fell
> among thieves, which stripped him of his raiment, and wounded
> him, and departed, leaving him half dead.
>
> And by chance there came down a certain priest that way; and
> when he saw him, he passed by on the other side.
>
> And likewise a Levite, when he was at the place, came and
> looked on him, and passed by on the other side.
>
> But a certain Samaritan, as he journeyed, came where he was;
> and when he saw him he had compassion on him.
>
> And went to him, and bound up his wounds, pouring in oil and
> wine, and set him on his own beast, and brought him to an inn,
> and took care of him.
>
> And on the morrow, when he departed, he took out two pence,
> and gave them to the host, and said unto him, "Take care of him;
> and whatsoever thou spendest more, when I come again, I will
> repay thee."   (Luke 10:30-35)

The Good Samaritan went out of his way, at some cost to himself, to
help one in need of it. We are not told what the options were, that is,
whether or not the priest and the Levite could have helped by doing
less than the Good Samaritan did, but assuming they could have, then
the fact they did nothing at all shows they were not even Minimally
Decent Samaritans, not because they were not Samaritans, but
because they were not even minimally decent.

These things are a matter of degree, of course, but there is a difference, and it comes out perhaps most clearly in the story of Kitty
Genovese, who, as you will remember, was murdered while thirty-
eight people watched or listened, and did nothing at all to help her.
A Good Samaritan would have rushed out to give direct assistance

against the murderer. Or perhaps we had better allow that it would have been a Splendid Samaritan who did this, on the ground that it would have involved a risk of death for himself. But the thirty-eight not only did not do this, they did not even trouble to pick up a phone to call the police. Minimally Decent Samaritanism would call for doing at least that, and their not having done it was monstrous.

After telling the story of the Good Samaritan, Jesus said "Go, and do thou likewise." Perhaps he meant that we are morally required to act as the Good Samaritan did. Perhaps he was urging people to do more than is morally required of them. At all events it seems plain that it was not morally required of any of the thirty-eight that he rush out to give direct assistance at the risk of his own life, and that it is not morally required of anyone that he give long stretches of his life—nine years or nine months—to sustaining the life of a person who has no special right (we were leaving open the possibility of this) to demand it.

Indeed, with one rather striking class of exceptions, no one in any country in the world is *legally* required to do anywhere near as much as this for anyone else. The class of exceptions is obvious. My main concern here is not the state of the law in respect to abortion, but it is worth drawing attention to the fact that in no state in this country is any man compelled by law to be even a Minimally Decent Samaritan to any person; there is no law under which charges could be brought against the thirty-eight who stood by while Kitty Genovese died. By contrast, in most states in this country women are compelled by law to be not merely Minimally Decent Samaritans, but Good Samaritans to unborn persons inside them. This doesn't by itself settle anything one way or the other, because it may well be argued that there should be laws in this country—as there are in many European countries—compelling at least Minimally Decent Samaritanism.[8] But it does show that there is a gross injustice in the existing state of the law. And it shows also that the groups currently working against liberalization of abortion laws, in fact working toward having it declared unconstitu-

8. For a discussion of the difficulties involved, and a survey of the European experience with such laws, see *The Good Samaritan and the Law*, ed. James M. Ratcliffe (New York, 1966).

tional for a state to permit abortion, had better start working for the
adoption of Good Samaritan laws generally, or earn the charge that
they are acting in bad faith.

I should think, myself, that Minimally Decent Samaritan laws
would be one thing, Good Samaritan laws quite another, and in fact
highly improper. But we are not here concerned with the law. What
we should ask is not whether anybody should be compelled by law to
be a Good Samaritan, but whether we must accede to a situation in
which somebody is being compelled—by nature, perhaps—to be a Good
Samaritan. We have, in other words, to look now at third-party interventions. I have been arguing that no person is morally required to
make large sacrifices to sustain the life of another who has no right
to demand them, and this even where the sacrifices do not include
life itself; we are not morally required to be Good Samaritans or anyway Very Good Samaritans to one another. But what if a man cannot
extricate himself from such a situation? What if he appeals to us to
extricate him? It seems to me plain that there are cases in which we
can, cases in which a Good Samaritan would extricate him. There you
are, you were kidnapped, and nine years in bed with that violinist lie
ahead of you. You have your own life to lead. You are sorry, but you
simply cannot see giving up so much of your life to the sustaining of
his. You cannot extricate yourself, and ask us to do so. I should have
thought that—in light of his having no right to the use of your body—
it was obvious that we do not have to accede to your being forced to
give up so much. We can do what you ask. There is no injustice to the
violinist in our doing so.

7. Following the lead of the opponents of abortion, I have throughout been speaking of the fetus merely as a person, and what I have
been asking is whether or not the argument we began with, which proceeds only from the fetus' being a person, really does establish its conclusion. I have argued that it does not.

But of course there are arguments and arguments, and it may be
said that I have simply fastened on the wrong one. It may be said that
what is important is not merely the fact that the fetus is a person,
but that it is a person for whom the woman has a special kind of
responsibility issuing from the fact that she is its mother. And it might
be argued that all my analogies are therefore irrelevant—for you do

not have that special kind of responsibility for that violinist, Henry Fonda does not have that special kind of responsibility for me. And our attention might be drawn to the fact that men and women both *are* compelled by law to provide support for their children.

I have in effect dealt (briefly) with this argument in section 4 above; but a (still briefer) recapitulation now may be in order. Surely we do not have any such "special responsibility" for a person unless we have assumed it, explicitly or implicitly. If a set of parents do not try to prevent pregnancy, do not obtain an abortion, and then at the time of birth of the child do not put it out for adoption, but rather take it home with them, then they have assumed responsibility for it, they have given it rights, and they cannot *now* withdraw support from it at the cost of its life because they now find it difficult to go on providing for it. But if they have taken all reasonable precautions against having a child, they do not simply by virtue of their biological relationship to the child who comes into existence have a special responsibility for it. They may wish to assume responsibility for it, or they may not wish to. And I am suggesting that if assuming responsibility for it would require large sacrifices, then they may refuse. A Good Samaritan would not refuse—or anyway, a Splendid Samaritan, if the sacrifices that had to be made were enormous. But then so would a Good Samaritan assume responsibility for that violinist; so would Henry Fonda, if he is a Good Samaritan, fly in from the West Coast and assume responsibility for me.

8. My argument will be found unsatisfactory on two counts by many of those who want to regard abortion as morally permissible. First, while I do argue that abortion is not impermissible, I do not argue that it is always permissible. There may well be cases in which carrying the child to term requires only Minimally Decent Samaritanism of the mother, and this is a standard we must not fall below. I am inclined to think it a merit of my account precisely that it does *not* give a general yes or a general no. It allows for and supports our sense that, for example, a sick and desperately frightened fourteen-year-old schoolgirl, pregnant due to rape, may *of course* choose abortion, and that any law which rules this out is an insane law. And it also allows for and supports our sense that in other cases resort to abortion is even positively indecent. It would be indecent in the woman to request an

abortion, and indecent in a doctor to perform it, if she is in her seventh month, and wants the abortion just to avoid the nuisance of postponing a trip abroad. The very fact that the arguments I have been drawing attention to treat all cases of abortion, or even all cases of abortion in which the mother's life is not at stake, as morally on a par ought to have made them suspect at the outset.

Secondly, while I am arguing for the permissibility of abortion in some cases, I am not arguing for the right to secure the death of the unborn child. It is easy to confuse these two things in that up to a certain point in the life of the fetus it is not able to survive outside the mother's body; hence removing it from her body guarantees its death. But they are importantly different. I have argued that you are not morally required to spend nine months in bed, sustaining the life of that violinist; but to say this is by no means to say that if, when you unplug yourself, there is a miracle and he survives, you then have a right to turn round and slit his throat. You may detach yourself even if this costs him his life; you have no right to be guaranteed his death, by some other means, if unplugging yourself does not kill him. There are some people who will feel dissatisfied by this feature of my argument. A woman may be utterly devastated by the thought of a child, a bit of herself, put out for adoption and never seen or heard of again. She may therefore want not merely that the child be detached from her, but more, that it die. Some opponents of abortion are inclined to regard this as beneath contempt—thereby showing insensitivity to what is surely a powerful source of despair. All the same, I agree that the desire for the child's death is not one which anybody may gratify, should it turn out to be possible to detach the child alive.

At this place, however, it should be remembered that we have only been pretending throughout that the fetus is a human being from the moment of conception. A very early abortion is surely not the killing of a person, and so is not dealt with by anything I have said here.

ROGER WERTHEIMER   Understanding
the Abortion Argument

I want to understand an argument. By an argument I do not mean a
concatenation of deathless propositions, but something with two sides
that you have with someone, not present to him; not something with
logical relations alone, but something encompassing human relations
as well. We need to understand the argument in this fuller sense, for
if we don't understand the human relations, we won't understand the
logical ones either. For data I use a fair share of the published mate-
rial plus intensive discussions with some two hundred students.[1] Here
too, if we don't understand what people actually say and do, we shall
never understand what they ought to say and do.

The argument is over the legalization of abortion. In its moral, as
opposed to, say, its political or medical aspects, the issue is statable
as a double-barreled question: At what stage of fetal development, if
any, and for what reasons, if any, is abortion justifiable? Each part of
the question has received diverse answers, which in turn have been
combined in various ways. Thus, we have not a single argument but
many, so I must subject them to considerable summary and simplifi-
cation in order to handle the larger issues.

Let me list a few popular positions. According to the liberal, the
fetus should be disposable upon the mother's request until it is viable;
thereafter it may be destroyed only to save the mother's life. To an extreme liberal the fetus is always merely *pars viscerum matris*, like an

1. My thanks to Mrs. Marilyn Weaver of the Oregon Committee on Legal
Termination of Pregnancy for providing much of the literature, and to Portland
State University for providing the students.

appendix, and may be destroyed upon demand anytime before its birth. In effect, this view denies that abortion ever needs any justification at all. A moderate view is that until viability the fetus should be disposable if it is the result of felonious intercourse, or if the mother's or child's physical or mental health would probably be gravely impaired. This position is susceptible to wide variations. For example, it can be liberalized by giving more weight to the reasonably foreseeable consequences of the pregnancy for the family as a whole. The conservative position is that the fetus may be aborted before quickening but not after, unless the mother's life is at stake. For the extreme conservative, the fetus, once conceived, may not be destroyed for any reason short of saving the mother's life.

This last might be called the Catholic view, but note that it, or some close variant of it, is shared by numerous Christian sects, and is or was maintained by Jews, by Indians of both hemispheres, by a variety of tribes of diverse geographical location and cultural level, and even by some contemporary atheistical biochemists who are political liberals. Much the same can be said of any of the listed positions. I call attention to such facts for two reasons. First, they suggest that the abortion issue is in some way special, since, given any position on abortion and any position on any other issue, you can probably find a substantial group of people, many of whom are rational and intelligent, who have simultaneously held both. Second, these facts are regularly denied or distorted by the disputants. Thus, liberals habitually argue as though extreme conservatism were an invention of contemporary scholasticism with a mere century of popish heritage behind it. This in the face of the fact that that position has had the force of law in most American states for more than a century, and continues to be law even in states where Catholicism is without influence. But why should liberals want to deny that conservatism can be freed from the peculiarities of Romanist theology and from religious belief altogether? After all, wouldn't the liberal critique be even more devastating if it located the true source of its adversary's beliefs and tore those beliefs up by their roots? We shall see that these two points are not unrelated.

Now, it is commonly said that the crux of the controversy is a disagreement as to the *value* of fetal life in its various stages. But I submit that this subtly but seriously misdescribes the actual arguments, and, further, betrays a questionable understanding of morality and perhaps a questionable morality as well. Instead, I suggest, we had best take the fundamental question to be: When does a human life begin?

First off I should note that the expressions "a human life," "a human being," "a person" are virtually interchangeable in this context. As I use these expressions, except for monstrosities, every member of our species is indubitably a person, a human being, at the very latest at birth. The question is whether we are human lives at any time before birth. Virtually everyone, at least every party to the current controversy, *actually* does agree to this. However, we should be aware that in this area both agreement and disagreement are often merely verbal and therefore only apparent. For example, many people will *say* that it takes a month or perhaps a year or even more after birth for the infant to become a person, and they will explain themselves by saying that a human being must have self-consciousness, or a personality, or be able to recognize and consciously interact with its environment. But upon investigation this disagreement normally turns out to be almost wholly semantic, for we can agree on all the facts about child development, and furthermore we can agree, at least in a general way, in our moral judgments on the care to be accorded the child at various stages. Thus, though they deny that a day-old infant is a person, they admit that its life cannot be forfeited for any reason that would not equally apply to a two-year-old.[2] Still, some substantive disagreements may separate myself from someone who is disinclined to call a neonate a person, but they are subtler than any I can encompass here.

On the other hand, significant disagreements can be masked by a merely verbal agreement. Sometimes a liberal will grant that a previable fetus is a human being, but investigation reveals that he means only that the fetus is a potential human being. Often he will flatly say

2. Granted, some societies practice infanticide, but their members are not parties to the present abortion dispute. And granted, further, in many of our jurisdictions infanticide, the murder of the young infant by its mother, is not punished as severely as other murders. However, this seems to be a function of our compassionate understanding of the anxiety and trauma attending the first months of motherhood; if a stranger kills the infant, the act is treated simply as murder.

that he calls it a human being because it would *become* a human being, thereby evidencing an ambiguity in his use of that expression. Or he may call it human to distinguish it from canine and feline fetuses, and call it alive or living in opposition to dead or inert. But this much can be said of any cells of the maternal organism, and the sum of these parts does not equal what he means when he uses the phrase "a human life" in connection with himself and his friends, for in that extended sense he could equally apply that expression to human terata, and, at least in extreme cases, he is inclined to deny that they are human lives, and to dispose of them accordingly.

Implicit in my remarks is the suggestion that one way to find out how someone uses the expression "human being" and related ones is by looking at his moral judgments. I am suggesting that this is a way, sometimes the only way, of learning both what someone means by such expressions and what his conception of a human being is. So, I am tempted to call our concept of a human being a moral concept—but I wouldn't know quite what I meant if I said that. Let me put it in more manageable, if somewhat vague, terms. It seems clear enough, at least in outline, that given that a man has a certain set of desires, we can discern his conception of something, X, by seeing what kinds of behavior he takes to be appropriate regarding X. I am saying that we may have to look at his *moral* beliefs regarding X, especially if X is a human being. And I want to say further that while some moral judgments are involved in determining whether the fetus is a human being, still, the crucial question about the fetus is not "How much is it worth?" but "What is it?" Admittedly, so far this is all horribly obscure. To get some clarity we must start examining the details of the abortion argument.

The defense of the extreme conservative position, as normally stated by Catholics, runs as follows. The key premise is that a human fetus is a human being, not a partial or potential one, but a full-fledged, actualized human life. Given that premise, the entire conservative position unfolds with a simple, relentless logic, every principle of which would be endorsed by any sensible liberal. Suppose human embryos are human beings. Their innocence is beyond question, so nothing could justify our destroying them except, perhaps, the necessity of saving some other innocent human life. That is, since similar cases must be treated in similar ways, some consideration would justify the abortion of a prenatal child if and only if a comparable consideration would justify the killing of a postnatal child.[3]

This is a serious and troubling argument posing an objection in principle to abortion. It is the *only* such argument. Nothing else could possibly justify the staggering social costs of the present abortion laws. Once the Catholic premise is granted, a liberal could reasonably dissent on only three side issues, none of which is a necessary or essential feature of conservatism.[4]

It should be unmistakably obvious what the Catholic position is. Yet, and this deserves heavy emphasis, liberals seem not to understand it, for their arguments are almost invariably infelicitous. The Catholic defense of the status quo is left unfazed, even untouched, by the standard liberal critique that consists of an inventory of the calamitous effects of our abortion laws on mother and child, on family, and on society in general. Of course, were it not for those effects we would feel no press to be rid of the laws—nor any *need* to retain them. That inventory does present a conclusive rebuttal of any of the piddling objections conservatives often toss in for good measure. But still, the

3. For brevity, I use an oversimplification of the principle against killing persons. Further refinements are otiose here, because, whatever they are, the issue remains whether they are to be applied equally to prenatal and postnatal humans.

4. The first concerns the Church's use of what is called the principle of double effect, which, when applied to some special obstetrical circumstances, implies that the doctor must let the mother die if his only alternative is intentionally killing the unborn child. Jonathan Bennett ("Whatever the Consequences," *Analysis* 26, no. 3 [1966]: 83-102) and Philippa Foot ("The Problem of Abortion and the Doctrine of the Double Effect," *Oxford Review* 5 [1967]: 5-15) have, I think, shown the principle to be ultimately indefensible, but in the process they make it seem to be more enlightened and to encapsulate many more insights than liberals have credited. At any rate, the principle has ceased to have much bearing on abortion cases because medical technology usually prevents the relevant circumstances from arising. Another spot at which a liberal could diverge from a Catholic is in the particular decisions regarding the degree of deformity required to warrant the destruction of the offspring. Since the nature of this dispute is much the same as that concerning the fetus, separate discussion would prove redundant. Lastly, a liberal could argue that human beings—of whatever age—can be blamelessly killed in more circumstances than Catholics concede. (Cf. note 3.) But clearly, any conservative concessions here would lend little comfort to liberals, since even liberals are reluctant to be very permissive about such principles.

precise, scientific tabulations of grief do not add up to an argument here, for sometimes pain, no matter how considerable and how undesirable, may not be avoidable, may not stem from some injustice. I do not intend to understate that pain; the tragedies brought on by unwanted children are plentiful and serious—but so too are those brought on by unwanted parents, yet few liberals would legalize parricide as the final solution to the massive social problem of the permanently visiting parent who drains his children's financial and emotional resources. In the Church's view, these cases are fully analogous: the fetus is as much a human life as is the parent; they share the same moral status. Either can be a source of abiding anguish and hardship for the other—and sometimes there may be no escape. In this, our world, some people get stuck with the care of others, and sometimes there may be no way of getting unstuck, at least no just and decent way. Taking the other person's life is not such a way.

The very elegance of the Catholic response is maddening. The ease with which it sweeps into irrelevance the whole catalogue of sorrow has incited many a liberal libel of the Catholic clergy as callous and unfeeling monsters, denied domestic empathy by their celibacy and the simplest human sympathies by their unnatural asceticism. Of course, slander is no substitute for argument—that's what the logic books say—and yet, we cast our aspersions with care, for they must deprive the audience of the *right* to believe the speaker. What wants explanation, then, is why the particular accusation of a *warped sensibility* seems, to the liberal, both just and pertinent. I shall come back to this. For the moment, it suffices to record that the liberal's accusation attests to a misunderstanding of the Catholic defense, for it is singularly inappropriate to label a man heartless who wants only to protect innocent human lives at all costs.

There is a subsidiary approach, a peculiarly liberal one, which seeks to disarm the Catholic position not by disputing it, but by conceding the Catholic's right to believe it and act accordingly. The liberal asks only that Catholics concede him the same freedom, and thus abandon support of abortion laws. To the liberal, the proposal is sweet reasonableness itself; the only demand is that Catholics be liberals—and when his offer is spurned, the depth of his exasperation measures the extent of his misunderstanding of the Catholic defense. The Catholic must retort that the issue is not, as the liberal supposes, one of religious ritual and self-regarding behavior, but of minority rights, the minority being not Catholics but the fetuses of all faiths, and the right being the right of an innocent human being to life itself. The liberal's proposal is predicated on abortion being a crime without a victim, like homosexuality or the use of contraceptives, but in the Catholic view the fetus is a full-scale victim and is so independent of the liberal's recognition of that fact. Catholics can no more think it wrong for themselves but permissible for Protestants to destroy a fetus than liberals can think it wrong for themselves but permissible for racists to victimize blacks. Given his premise, the Catholic is as justified in employing the power of the state to protect embryos as the liberal is to protect blacks. I shall be returning to this analogy, because the favored defense of slavery and discrimination, from Aristotle to the Civil War and beyond, takes the form of a claim that the subjugated creatures are by nature inferior to their masters, that they are *not fully human*.[5]

Now, why do liberals, even the cleverest ones, so consistently fail to make contact with the Catholic challenge?[6] After all, as I have made plain, once premised that the fetus is a person, the entire conservative position recites the common sense of any moral man. The liberal's failure is, I suggest, due to that premise, not to some Jesuitical subtlety in the reasoning. It is the liberal's imagination, not his intellect, that is boggled. He doesn't know how to respond to the argument, because he cannot *make sense* of that premise. To him, it is not simply

5. A further instance of the liberal's befuddlement: for the Catholic, not only must a Catholic—or non-Catholic—doctor refrain from performing an abortion, he must also refuse a patient's request for a referral to a doctor who would perform it. Liberals regularly rage against this as an additional outrage by the Church, but it is an additional part of the Church's position only in being distinct, not in being separable, since, if an act constitutes a grave wrong, surely it is wrong to aid and abet that act. If it is wrong to enslave a man, it is wrong to inform a master of the whereabouts of his fugitive slave, and also wrong to refer him to someone who would so inform.

6. I think it undeniable that some of the liberals' bungling can be dismissed as the unseemly sputterings and stutterings of a transparently camouflaged anti-Catholic bias—but not all of it can.

false, but wildly, madly false; it is nonsense, totally unintelligible, literally unbelievable. Just look at an embryo. It is an amorphous speck of apparently coagulated protoplasm. It has no eyes or ears, no head at all. It can't walk or talk; you can't dress it or wash it. Why, it doesn't even qualify as a Barbie doll, and yet millions of people call it a human being, just like one of us. It's as though someone were to look at an acorn and call it an oak tree, or, better, it's as though someone squirted a paint tube at a canvas and called the outcome a painting, a work of art—and people believed him. The whole thing is precisely that mad—and just that sane. The liberal is befuddled by the conservative's argument, just as Giotto would be were he to assess a Pollock production as a *painting*. If the premises make no sense, then neither will the rest of the argument, except as an exercise in abstract logic—and that is, I think, the only way in which liberals do understand the conservative argument.

The Catholic claim would be a joke were it not that millions of people take it seriously, and millions more suffer for their solemnity. Liberals need an explanation of how it is possible for the conservatives to believe what they say, for after all, conservatives are not ignorant or misinformed about the facts here—I mean, for example, the facts of embryology. To be sure, both camps have their complement of the benighted, but then again, neither side has a monopoly on competent doctors. It's not as though the antiabortionists thought embryos were homunculi in the mother's belly, just like us, only much, much smaller. If they thought something like that (and, in fact, at one time some of them did) then perhaps the liberal could understand them and dismiss their ravings with the aid of an electron microscope. So the liberal asks, "How *can* they believe what they say? How *can* they even make sense of it?" The question is forced upon the liberal because his conception of rationality is jeopardized by the possibility that a normal, unbiased observer of the relevant facts could really accept the conservative claim. It is this question, I think, that drives the liberal to attribute the whole antiabortion movement to Catholicism and to the Roman clergy in particular. For it is comforting to suppose that the conservative beliefs could take root only in a mind that had been carefully cultivated since infancy to support every extravagant dogma of an arcane theology fathered by the victims of unnatural and

unhealthy lives.[7] But, discomforting though it may be, people, and
not just Catholics, can and sometimes do agree on all the facts about
embryos and still disagree as to whether they are persons. Indeed,
apparently people can agree on *every* fact and still disagree on
whether it is a fact that embryos are human beings. So now one might
begin to wonder: What sort of fact is it?

I hasten to add that not only can both parties agree on the scientific facts, they need not disagree on any supernatural facts either.
The situation here is *not* comparable to that in which a man stands
before what looks for all the world like some fermented grape juice
and a biscuit and calls it the blood and body of someone who died
and decomposed a couple of millennia ago. The conservative claim
does not presuppose that we are invested with a soul, some sort of
divine substance, at or shortly after our conception. No doubt it helps
to have one's mind befogged by visions of holy hocus-pocus, but it's
not necessary, since some unmuddled atheists endorse a demytholo-
gized Catholic view. Moreover, since ensoulment is an unverifiable
occurrence, the theologian dates it either by means of some revela-
tion—which, by the way, the Church does not (though some of its
parishioners may accept the humanity of embryos on the Church's
say-so)—or by means of the same scientifically acceptable data by
which his atheistical counterpart gauges the emergence of an unbe-
souled human life (e.g., that at such and such a time the organism
is capable of independent life, or is motile, or assumes human form,
or possesses its complete genetic makeup).

The religious position derives its plausibility from independent secular considerations. It serves as an expression of them, not as a substitute for them. In brief, here as elsewhere, talk about souls involves
an unnecessary shuffle. Yet, though unnecessary, admittedly it is not

7. Consequently, liberals deprive themselves of any genuine understanding of
that theology by overlooking its natural attractions, which are considerable. Not
a few liberals have eagerly believed that the Church's population policy was
designed by devilishly clever bishops questing after worldly wealth and power
via a burgeoning Catholic horde. So, it is left a mystery as perturbing as the
Trinity why the wily Romanists insist that the heathen numbers keep pace, and
why they persist in their plot in spite of the fact, oft-noted by liberals, that the
continuing overpopulation of Catholic countries perpetuates their poverty and
impotence.

without effect, for such conceptions color our perceptions and attitudes toward the world and thereby give sense and substance to certain arguments whose secular translations lack appeal. To take a pertinent instance, the official Church position (not the one believed by most of the laity or used against the liberals, but the official position) is that precisely because ensoulment is an unverifiable occurrence, we can't locate it with certainty, and hence abortion at any stage involves the *risk* of destroying a human life. But first off, it is doubtful whether this claim can support the practical conclusions the Catholic draws. For even if it is true, is abortion an *unwarrantable* risk? Always? Is it morally indefensible to fire a pistol into an uninspected barrel? After all, a child *might* be hiding in it. Secondly, though this argument has no attractive secular version, still, it derives its appeal from profane considerations. For what is it that so much as makes it seem that a blastocyst *might* be a person? If the conception of being besouled is cut loose from the conception of being human sans soul, then a human soul might reside in anything at all (or at least any living thing), and then the destruction of anything (or any living thing) would involve the risk of killing someone. This picture of the world is quite alien to the rationalist tradition of Catholicism, but some Eastern religions have adopted it, and the course of life appropriate to it. Not surprisingly, that course of life seems madly inefficient and irrational to Western liberals.

I have said that the argument from risk has no secular counterpart. But why not? Well, for example, what sense would it make to the liberal to suppose that an embryo *might* be a person? Are there any discoveries that are really (not just logically) possible which would lead him to admit he was mistaken? It is not a *hypothesis* for the liberal that embryos are not persons; *mutatis mutandis* for the conservative, who might well say of the fetus: "My attitude towards him is an attitude towards a soul. I am not of the *opinion* that he has a soul."[8]

At this juncture of the argument, a liberal with a positivistic background will announce that the whole dispute is not over a matter of fact at all; it's just a matter of definition whether the fetus is a person. If by this the liberal means that the question "Is a fetus a person?" is

8. Ludwig Wittgenstein, *Philosophical Investigations*, trans. G.E.M. Anscombe (New York, 1953), p. 178e.

equivalent to "Is it proper to call a fetus a person?"—that is, "Is it true
to say of a fetus, 'It is a person'?"—then the liberal is quite right and
quite unhelpful. But he is likely to add that we can define words any
way we like. And that is either true and unhelpful or flatly false. For
note, both liberals and conservatives think it wrong to kill an innocent
person except when other human lives would be lost. So neither party
will reform their speech habits regarding the fetus unless that moral
principle is reworded in a way that vouchsafes their position on abortion. Any stipulated definition can be recommended only by appealing
to the very matters under dispute. Any such definition will therefore
fail of universal acceptance and thus only mask the real issues, unless
it is a mere systematic symbol switch. In brief, agreement on a definition will be a consequence of, not a substitute for, agreement on the
facts.

A more sophisticated liberal may suggest that fetuses are borderline
cases. Asking whether fetuses are persons is like asking whether
viruses are living creatures: the proper answer is that they are like
them in some ways but not in others; the rules of the language don't
dictate one way or the other, so you can say what you will. Yet this
suggests that we share a single concept of a human being, one with
a fuzzy or multifaceted boundary that would make any normal person
feel indecision about whether a fetus is a human being, and would
enable that person, however he decided, to understand readily how
someone else might decide otherwise. But at best this describes only
the minds of moderates. Liberals and conservatives suffer little indecision, and, further, they are enigmatic to one another, both intellec-
tually and as whole persons. The liberal can neither understand nor
believe in the conservative's horror of abortion, especially when the
conservative then so blithely accepts the consequences of prohibiting
the operation. In turn, the conservative is baffled by and mistrustful
of the liberal who welcomes abortion with an easy equanimity and
then agonizes his soul so mightily over the poignant dilemma posed by
Ivan Karamazov to Alyosha ("Rebellion"). Each side suspects the
other of schizoid derangement or self-serving hypocrisy or both. And
finally, precisely because with the virus you can say what you will, it
is unlike the fetus. As regards the virus, scientists can manage nicely
while totally ignoring the issue. Not so with the fetus, because decid-

ing what to call it is tantamount to a serious and unavoidable moral decision.

This last remark suggests that the fetus' humanity is really a moral issue, not a factual one at all. This suggestion would sit well with the positivistically minded liberals, since for them it would explain how there could be unanimity on every issue except whether a fetus is a person. But I submit that if one insists on using that raggy fact-value distinction, then one ought to say that the dispute is over a matter of fact in the sense in which it is a fact that the Negro slaves were human beings. But it would be better to say that this dispute calls that distinction into question. To see this, let us look at how people actually argue about when a human life begins.

The liberal dates hominization from birth or viability. The choice of either stage is explicable by reference to some obvious considerations. At birth the child leaves its own private space and enters the public world. He becomes an active member of the community, a physically separate and distinct individual. He begins to act and behave like a human being, not just move as he did in the womb. And he can be looked at and acted upon and interacted with. He has needs and wants independent from those of his mother. And so on. On the other hand, someone may say viability is the crucial point, because it is then that the child has the capacity to do all those things it does at birth; the sole difference is a quite inessential one of geography.

Now note about both of these sets of considerations that they are not used as proofs or parts of proofs that human life begins at birth or at viability. What would the major premise of such a proof be? The liberal does not—nor does anyone else—have a rule of the language or a definition of "human life" from which it follows that if the organism has such and such properties, then it is a human life. True, some people, especially some scholastically oriented Catholics, have tried to state the essence of human life and argue from that definition, but the correctness of any such definition must first be tested against our judgments of particular cases, and on some of those judgments people disagree; so the argument using such a definition which tries to settle that disagreement can only beg the question. Thus, it seems more accurate to say simply that the kinds of considerations I have mentioned explain why the liberal chooses to date human life in a certain way. More accurately still, I don't think the liberal chooses or decides at all; rather, he looks at certain facts and he responds in a particular way to those facts: he dates human life from birth or from viability—and he acts and feels accordingly.[9] There is nothing surprising in such behavior, nor anything irrational or illegitimate.

All this can be said of any of the considerations that have been used to mark the beginning of a human life. Quickening—that is, when the mother first *feels* the fetus move—could be used, because that clearly serves as a sign of life. Liberal detractors point out that the fetus moves long before the mother feels it, and biologically it is a living organism long before that. But such objections overlook the connections between our concept of a person and our concept of an agent, something that can act. It's not to be wondered at that quickening should seem a dramatic moment, especially to the mother who receives the fetus' signal that it *can now move on its own.*

Similarly, liberals always misplace the attractions of fertilization as the critical date when they try to argue that if you go back that far, you could just as well call the sperm or the egg a human being. But people call the zygote a human life not just because it contains the DNA blueprint which determines the physical development of the organism from then on, and not just because of the potential inherent in it, but also because it and it alone can claim to be the beginning of the spatio-temporal-causal chain of the physical object that is a human body. And though I think the abortion controversy throws doubt on the claim that bodily continuity is the *sole* criterion of personal identity, I think the attractions of that philosophical thesis are of a piece with the attractions of fertilization as the point marking the start of a person. Given our conceptual framework, one can't go back further. Neither the sperm nor the egg could be, by itself, a human being, any more than an atom of sodium or an atom of chlorine could by itself properly be called salt. One proof of this is that *no one* is in the least inclined to call a sperm or an egg a human life, a fact acknowledged by the liberal's very argument, which has the form of a *reductio ad absurdum.* At one time people were so inclined, but only because they thought the sperm merely triggered the develop-

9. His response has cognitive, behavioral, and affective aspects. I make no suggestion regarding their temporal or causal relations.

ment of the egg and hence the egg was a human being, or they thought that the egg was merely the seedbed for the male seed and thus the sperm was a human being.

One other dating deserves mention, since, though rarely stated, it is often used, especially by moderates: the period during which the fetus takes on a recognizably human form, the period when it begins to *look* human. The appeal of this is conveyed by Wittgenstein's remark: "The human body is the best picture of the human soul."[10]

These are some of the considerations, but how are they actually presented? What, for example, does the liberal say and do? Note that his arguments are usually formulated as a series of rhetorical questions. He points to certain facts, and then, quite understandably, he expects his listeners to respond in a particular way—and when they don't, he finds their behavior incomprehensible. First he will point to an infant and say, "Look at it! Aren't you inclined to say that it is one of us?" And then he will describe an embryo as I did earlier, and say, "Look at the difference between it and us! Could you call that a human being?" All this is quite legitimate, but notice what the liberal is doing. First, he has us focus our attention on the *earliest stages* of the fetus, where the contrast with us is greatest. He does not have us look at the fetus shortly before viability or birth, where the differences between it and what he is willing to call a human being are quite minimal. Still, this is not an unfair tactic when combating the view that the fertilized egg is a human life. The other side of this maneuver is that he has us compare the embryo with *us adults.* This seems fair in that we are our own best paradigms of a person. If you and I aren't to be called human beings, then what is? And yet the liberal would not say that a young child or a neonate or even a viable fetus is to be called a human life only in an extended sense. He wants to say that the infant at birth or the viable fetus is a one-hundred-percent human being, but, again, the differences between a neonate and a viable fetus or between a viable fetus and a soon-to-be-viable fetus are not impressive.

The liberal has one other arrow in his meager quiver. He will say that if you call an embryo a human life, then presumably you think

10. *Philosophical Investigations*, p. 178e.

it is a valuable entity. But, he adds, what does it have that is of any value? Its biochemical potential to become one of us doesn't ensure that it itself is of any real value, especially if neither the mother nor any other interested party wants it to fulfill that potential. Besides, it's not as though zygotes were rare; they're all too plentiful, and normally it's no great hardship to mix another batch. And don't tell me that the zygote is of great worth because it has a divine soul, for you can't even show that such things exist, let alone that *this* entity has one.

When liberals say that an embryo is of no value if no one has a good reason to want to do anything but destroy it, I think they are on firm ground. But the conservative is not saying that the embryo has some really nifty property, so precious that it's a horrid waste to destroy it. No, he is saying that the embryo is a human being and it is wrong to kill human beings, and that is why you must not destroy the embryo. The conservative realizes that, unless he uses religious premises, premises inadmissible in the court of common morality, he has no way of categorically condemning the killing of a fetus except by arguing that a fetus is a person. And he doesn't call it a human being because its properties are valuable. The properties it has which make it a human being may be valuable, but he does not claim that it is their value which makes it a human being. Rather, he argues that it is a human being by turning the liberal's argument inside out.

The conservative points, and keeps pointing, to the similarities between each set of successive stages of fetal development, instead of pointing, as the liberal does, to the gross differences between widely separated stages. Each step of his argument is persuasive, but if this were all there was to it, his total argument would be no more compelling than one which traded on the fuzziness of the boundaries of baldness and the arbitrariness of any sharp line of demarcation to conclude that Richard M. Nixon is glabrous. If this were the whole conservative argument, then it would be open to the liberal's *reductio* argument, which says that if you go back as far as the zygote, the sperm and the egg must also be called persons. But in fact the conservative can stop at the zygote; fertilization does seem to be a nonarbitrary point marking the inception of a particular object, a human body. That is, the conservative has *independent* reasons for picking the date of conception, just like the liberal who picks the date of birth or viability, and unlike the sophist who concludes that Nixon is bald.

But we still don't have the whole conservative argument, for on the basis of what has been said so far the conservative should also call an acorn an oak tree, but he doesn't, and the reason he uses is that, as regards a human life, it would be *morally* arbitrary to use any date other than that of conception. That is, he can ask liberals to name the earliest stage at which they are willing to call the organism a human being, something which may not be killed for any reason short of saving some other human life. The conservative will then take the stage of development immediately preceding the one the liberals choose and challenge them to point to a difference between the two stages, a difference that is a morally relevant difference, a difference that would justify the massive moral and legal difference of allowing us to kill the creature at the earlier stage while prohibiting that same act at the succeeding stage.

Suppose the liberal picks the date of birth. Yet a newborn infant is only a fetus that has suffered a change of address and some physiological changes like respiration. A neonate delivered in its twenty-fifth week lies in an incubator physically less well developed and no more independent than a normal fetus in its thirty-seventh week in the womb. What difference is there that justifies calling that neonate a person, but not that fetus? What difference is there that can be used to justify killing the prenatal child where it would be wrong to kill the postnatal child?

Or suppose the liberal uses the date of viability. But the viability of a fetus is its capacity to survive outside the mother, and *that* is totally relative to the state of the available medical technology. At present the law dates viability from the twenty-eighth week, but so late a date is now without any medical justification. In principle, eventually the fetus may be deliverable at any time, perhaps even at conception. The problems this poses for liberals are obvious, and in fact one finds that either a liberal doesn't understand what viability really is, so that he takes it to be necessarily linked to the later fetal stages; or he is an extreme liberal in disguise, who is playing along with the first kind of liberal for political purposes; or he has abandoned the viability criterion and is madly scurrying about in search of some other factor in the late fetal stages which might serve as a nonarbitrary cutoff point. For example, in recent years some liberals have been purveying pious nonsense about the developing cerebral cortex in the third trimester and its relation to consciousness. But I am inclined to suppose that the conservative is right, that going back stage by stage from the infant to the zygote one will not find any differences between successive stages significant enough to bear the enormous moral burden of allowing wholesale slaughter at the earlier stage while categorically denying that permission at the next stage.

It needs to be stressed here that we are talking about life and death on a colossal scale. It has been estimated that thirty million abortions are performed yearly, one million in the United States alone. So the situation contrasts sharply with that in which a society selects a date like the eighteenth or twenty-first birthday on which to confer certain legal rights, for the social costs of using a less arbitrary measure of maturity can reasonably be held to outweigh any injustices involved in the present system. Even the choice of a birthday for military conscription, a morally ambiguous practice anyway, is not comparable for obvious reasons.

The full power and persuasiveness of the conservative argument is still not revealed until we uncover its similarities to and connections with any of the dialectical devices that have been used to widen a man's recognition of his fellowship with all the members of his biological species, regardless of their race or sex or nationality or religion or lineage or social class. To be sure, not every discriminatory injustice based on such arbitrary and morally irrelevant features as race or sex has been rationalized on the grounds that the victim is not a full-fledged human being. Still, it is a matter of record that men of good will have often failed to recognize that a certain class of fellow creatures were really human beings just like themselves.

To take but one example, the history of Negro slavery includes among the white oppressors men who were, in all other regards, essentially just and decent. Many such men sincerely defended their practice of slavery with the claim that the Negro was not a member of the moral community of men. Not only legally, but also conceptually, for the white master, the Negro was property, livestock. The manor lord could be both benevolent and unjust with a clear Christian conscience because he regarded the slave as some sort of demiperson, a blathering beast of burden. And given the white man's background, we can understand, if not sympathize with, his perception of Negroes. For either he had never seen one before, or he had been reared in a culture in which it was an accepted practice to treat and regard them, to talk about and perceive them in a certain way. That they were full-fledged human beings, the sort of creatures that it is wrong to kill or enslave, was a claim he found incredible. He would be inclined to, and actually did, simply point to the Negroes and say: "Look at them! Can't you see the differences between them and us?" And the fact is that at one time that argument had an undeniable power, as undeniable as the perceptual differences it appealed to. Check your own perceptions. Ask yourself whether you really, in a purely phenomenological sense, *see* a member of another race in the same way you see a member of your own. Why is it that all Chinamen look alike and are so inscrutable? Add to the physiological facts the staggering cultural disparities dividing slave and master, and you may start to sense the force of the master's argument. What has been the rebuttal? We point to the similarities between Negro and white, and then step by step describe the differences and show about each one that it is not a morally relevant difference, not the kind of difference that warrants enslaving or in any way discriminating against a Negro.

The parallels with the abortion controversy are palpable. Let me extend them some more. First, sometimes a disagreement over a creature's humanity does turn on beliefs about subsidiary matters of fact—but it need not. Further, when it does not, when the disagreement develops from differing responses to the same data, the issue is still a factual one and not a matter of taste. It is not that one party prefers or approves of or has a favorable attitude or emotion toward some property, while the other party does not. Our response concerns what the thing is, not whether we like it or whether it is good. And when I say I don't *care* about the color of a man's skin, that it's not *important* to me, I am saying something quite different than when I say I don't care about the color of a woman's hair. I am saying that this property cannot be used to justify discriminatory behavior or social arrangements. It cannot be so used because it is irrelevant; neither black skin nor white skin is, in and of itself, of any value. Skin color has no logical relation to the question of how to treat a man. The slaveholder's response is not that white skin is of intrinsic value. Rather, he replies that people with naturally black skins are niggers, and that is an inferior kind of creature. So too, the liberal does not claim that infants possess some intrinsically valuable attribute lacked by prenatal children. Rather, he says that a prenatal child is a fetus, not a human being.

In brief, when seen in its totality the conservative's argument *is* the liberal's argument turned completely inside out. While the liberal stresses the differences between disparate stages, the conservative stresses the resemblances between consecutive stages. The liberal asks, "What has a zygote got that is valuable?" and the conservative answers, "Nothing, but it's a human being, so it is wrong to abort it." Then the conservative asks, "What does a fetus lack that an infant has that is so valuable?" and the liberal answers, "Nothing, but it's a fetus, not a human being, so it is all right to abort it." The arguments are equally strong and equally weak, for they are the *same* argument, an argument that can be pointed in either of two directions. The argument does not itself point in either direction: it is *we* who must point it, and *we* who are led by it. If you are led in one direction rather than the other, that is not because of logic, but because you respond in a certain way to certain facts.

Recall that the arguments are usually formulated in the interrogative, not the indicative, mood. Though the answers are supposed to be absolutely obvious, they are not comfortably assertible. Why? Because an assertion is a truth claim which invites a request for a proof, but here any assertible proof presupposes premises which beg the question. If one may speak of proof here, it can lie only in the audience's response, in their acceptance of the answer and of its obviousness. The questions convince by leading us to appreciate familiar facts. The conclusion is validated not through assertible presuppositions, but through our acknowledgment that the questions are *rhetorical.* You might say that the conclusion is our seeing a certain aspect: e.g., we see the embryo as a human being. But this seems an unduly provocative description of the situation, for what is at issue is whether such an aspect is there to be seen.

Evidently, we have here a paradigm of what Wittgenstein had in mind when he spoke of the possibility of two people agreeing on the application of a rule for a long period, and then, suddenly and quite inexplicably, diverging in what they call going on in the same way. This possibility led him to insist that linguistic communication presupposes not only agreement in definitions, but also agreement in judgments, in what he called forms of life[11]—something that seems lacking in the case at hand. Apparently, the conclusion to draw is that it is not true that the fetus is a human being, but it is not false either. Without an agreement in judgments, without a common response to the pertinent data, the assertion that the fetus is a human being cannot be assigned a genuine truth-value.

Yet, we surely want to say that Negroes are and always have been full-fledged human beings, no matter what certain segments of mankind may have thought, and no matter how numerous or unanimous those segments were. The humanity of the slaves seems unlike that of the fetus, but not because by now a monolithic majority recognizes—however grudgingly—the full human status of Negroes, whereas no position regarding the fetus commands more than a plurality. The mere fact of disagreement in judgments or forms of life would not render unsettleable statements about the humanity of fetuses, otherwise the comparable statements about Negroes, or for that matter whites, would meet a similar fate. What seems special about the fetus is that, apparently, we have no vantage point from which to criticize opposing systems of belief.

It will be said by some that a form of life is a "given," "what has to be accepted,"[12] something not really criticizable by or from an opposing form of life. There are various long answers to that, but a couple of short ones should suffice here. First, it is also part of our form of life, and every other one I know of, that rational and justifiable criticisms of opposing forms of life can be and are made; it seems that that practice "has to be accepted" at face value as much as any other. Second, in this instance the point is without practical relevance, since

11. Caveat lector! The notion of a form of life is a swamp from whose bourn no philosopher has returned. I would fain forgo the well-known conceits of another had I but time and talent enow to conjure with my own.

12. Wittgenstein, *Philosophical Investigations*, p. 226e.

the differences between the disputants are not so systematic and entire
as to block every avenue of rational discussion. Clearly, their com-
munality is very great, their differences relatively isolated and free-
floating. Thus, for example, liberals and conservatives seem quite
capable of understanding this paper. At any rate, it would be self-
indulgent for me to take any disagreements they may have with me to
be evidence to the contrary.

At this stage of the dispute over a creature's humanity, I stand to
the slaveholder in roughly the same relation I stand to the color-blind
man who judges this sheet of paper to be gray. Our differing color
judgments express our differing immediate responses to the same
data. But his color judgment is mistaken because his vision is defective. I criticize his judgment by criticizing him, by showing him to be
abnormal, deviant—which is not the same as being in the minority.
In a like manner we criticize those basic beliefs and attitudes which
sanction and are sustained by the slaveholder's form of life. We argue
that his form of life is, so to speak, an accident of history, explicable
by reference to special socio-psychological circumstances that are
inessential to the natures of blacks and whites.[13] The fact that Negroes
can and, special circumstances aside, naturally *would* be regarded
and treated no differently than Caucasians is at once a necessary and
a sufficient condition for its being right to so regard and treat them.
Thus, while we may in large measure understand the life-style of the
slaveholder and perhaps withhold condemnation of the man, we need
not and should not condone his behavior.

Liberals and conservatives rail at each other with this same canoni-
cal schema. And if, for example, antiabortionism required the pervert-
ing of natural reason and normal sensibilities by a system of super-
stitions, then the liberal could discredit it—but it doesn't, so he can't.
As things stand, it is not at all clear what, if anything, is the normal
or natural or healthy response toward the fetus; it is not clear what is
to count as the special historical and social circumstances, which, if
removed, would leave us with the appropriate way to regard and treat

13. This point can be overstated. We develop our concept of a human through
our relations with those near us and like us, and thus, at least initially, an
isolated culture will generally perceive and describe foreigners as alien, strange,
and not foursquare human.

the fetus.[14] And I think that the unlimited possibility of natural *responses* is simply the other side of the fact of severely limited possibilities of natural *relationships* with the fetus. After all, there isn't much we can do with a fetus; either we let it out or we do it in. I have little hope of seeing a justification for doing one thing or the other unless this situation changes. As things stand, the range of interactions is so minimal that we are not compelled to regard the fetus in any particular way. For example, respect for a fetus cannot be wrung from us as respect for a Negro can be and is, unless we are irretrievably warped or stunted.

No doubt the assumptions behind these remarks are large and complex, but I take the essential points here to be bits of moral common sense, data to be understood, and, at least at the outset, accepted, not philosophical theses to be refuted. Of course, if we discredit certain *basic* beliefs because of their causal history, we may have to redefine the so-called genetic fallacy and reassess the work of Wittgenstein and others who treat as irrelevant to the validity of such basic beliefs the explanation of how and why we come to have them.[15] However that may be, we seem to be stuck with the indeterminateness of the fetus' humanity. This does not mean that, whatever you believe, it is true or true for you if you believe it. Quite the contrary, it means that,

14. I have heard many people say that they believe what they do about the fetus "because that's what I was brought up to believe." Of course this can't justify their belief, but it's also suspect as an explanation. Even if you acquired your belief by *learning*, it does not follow that you were *taught*. Ask yourself when were you taught and by whom that a human life begins at such and such a time—or have you repressed the memory of that terrifying scene? Have you told a child or seen it done? Many people (e.g., Catholics) are instructed on this matter, and many of them accept the teachings, but many people come to reject what they were taught. (Even contemporary Catholic theologians disagree.) How is that to be explained?

15. Incidentally, we might also stop balking at the *structure* of Nietzsche's critique of our morality, and start facing up to the *content* of his argument. One could concede the claim that our morality, our set of basic values is a *cause* of a sick (diseased, unhealthy, unnatural) mind (person, life, culture), for the claim leaves open whether certain values should be sacrificed for certain others. One cannot be so glib with the claim that our values are a *consequence* of our valetudinarian condition, for if the claim is granted the conclusion seems as inescapable as it is terrible. (Nietzsche spoke of "terrible truths.") Nietzsche may have made the first claim; he certainly made the second.

whatever you believe, it's not true—but neither is it false. You believe it, and that's the end of the matter.

But obviously that's not the end of the matter; the same urgent moral and political decisions still confront us. But before we run off to make our existential leaps over the liberal-conservative impasse, we might meander through the moderate position. I'll shorten the trip by speaking only of features found throughout the spectrum of moderate views. For the moderate, the fetus is not a human being, but it's not a mere maternal appendage either; it's a human fetus, and it has a separate moral status just as animals do. A fetus is not an object that we can treat however we wish, but neither is it a person whom we must treat as we would wish to be treated in return. Thus, *some* legal prohibitions on abortions *might* be justified in the name of the fetus qua human fetus, just as we accord some legal protection to animals, not for the sake of the owners, but for the benefit of the animals themselves.

The popularity of this position is, I believe, generally underestimated; ultimately, most liberals and conservatives are, in a sense, only extreme moderates. Few liberals really regard abortion, at least in the later stages, as a bit of elective surgery. Suppose a woman had her fifth-month fetus aborted purely out of curiosity as to what it looked like, and perhaps then had it bronzed. Who among us would not deem both her and her actions reprehensible? Or, to go from the lurid to the ludicrous, suppose a wealthy woman, a Wagner addict, got an abortion in her fourth month because she suddenly realized that she would come to term during the Bayreuth Festival. Only an exceptional liberal would not blanch at such behavior. Of course, in both cases one might refuse to outlaw the behavior, but still, clearly we do not respond to these cases as we would to the removal of an appendix or a tooth. Similarly, in my experience few of even the staunchest conservatives consistently regard the fetus, at least in the earlier stages, in the same way as they do a fellow adult. When the cause of grief is a miscarriage, the object of grief is the mother; rarely does anyone feel pity or sorrow for the embryo itself. So too, it is most unusual for someone to urge the same punishment for a mother who aborts a young fetus as for one who murders her grown child. Nevertheless, enough people give enough substance to the liberal and conservative positions to justify describing them as I have done, as views differing in kind rather than degree.[16]

The moderate position is as problematic as it is popular. (The virtue of compromise is mass appeal; coherence may not be a consideration.) The moderate is driven in two directions, liberalism and conservatism, by the very same question: Why do you make these exceptions and not those? Why, for example, single out incestuous offspring as unworthy of protection? Are they so tainted by a broken taboo, or is the exception based upon a general utilitarian consideration that would equally justify the mass of abortions that are actually desired?

The difficulty here is comparable to that regarding animals. There are dogs, pigs, mosquitoes, worms, bacteria, etc., and we kill them for food, clothing, ornamentation, sport, convenience, and out of simple irritation or unblinking inadvertence. We allow different animals to be killed for different reasons, and there are enormous differences between people on all of this. In general, for most of us, the higher the evolutionary stage of the species or the later the developmental stage of the fetus, the more restricted our permission to kill; the more a thing is like us—ontogenetically or phylogenetically—the more we are disposed to treat it like a human being. But it is far more complicated than that, and anyone with a fully consistent, let alone principled, system of beliefs on these matters is usually thought fanatical by the rest of us.

To stabilize his position, the moderate would have to *invent* a new set of moral categories and principles. A happy amalgamation of the ones we have won't do, because our principles of justice apply solely to the relations between persons,[17] and our concepts of zygote, embryo, and fetus are biological, not moral, categories. But *how* is one to

16. On the other hand, the above considerations suggest that the human status of a fetus is not indeterminate for the *whole* of its gestation.

17. An oversimplification whose import remains to be gauged. Compare: I stumble in the dark over my sleeping schnauzer; I stumble over my ottoman. To *blame* either nonperson is irrational; to blame the dog is also *unfair*, but to blame the furniture is neither fair nor unfair. So too: my bitch leaves me five pups. Without special reason it would be *unfair* to apportion the food unequally among them.

invent new categories and principles? I'm not sure it can be done, especially with the scanty building materials available. Again, our interactions with fetuses are extremely limited and peripheral, which is why our normative conceptual machinery in this area is so abbreviated, unformed, and up for grabs.

But perhaps this could be otherwise. Close your eyes for a moment and imagine that, due to advances in medical technology or mutation caused by a nuclear war, the relevant cutaneous and membranous shields became transparent from conception to parturition, so that when a mother put aside her modesty and her clothing the developing fetus would be in full public view. Or suppose instead, or in addition, that anyone could at any time pluck a fetus from its womb, air it, observe it, fondle it, and then stick it back in after a few minutes. And we could further suppose that this made for healthier babies, and so maybe laws would be passed requiring that it be done regularly. And we might also imagine that gestation took nine days rather than nine months. What then would we think of aborting a fetus? What would *you* think of aborting it? And what does that say about what you *now* think?

In my experience, when such imaginative exercises are properly presented people are often, not always, moved by them, different people by different stories. They begin to talk about all of it somewhat differently than they had before, and less differently from each other. However, the role of such conjectures in or as arguments is far from clear. I'm not sure whether people find out something about themselves, or change under the impact of their own imaginations, or both—one as a consequence of the other. I don't think we discover the justifications for our beliefs by such a procedure. A liberal who is disturbed by the picture of a transparent womb may be acquiring some self-knowledge; he may come to realize how much power being visible and being hidden have for us and for him, and he may make a connection between this situation and the differing experiences of an infantryman and a bombardier. But surely the fetus' being hidden was not the liberal's *reason* for thinking it expendable.

Nor is it evident that such *Gedanken* experiments reveal the causes of our beliefs. Their results seem too unreliable to provide anything but the grossest projections as to how we would in fact react in the imagined situations. When I present myself with such science fiction fantasies, I am inclined to respond as I do to a question posed by Hilary Putnam:[18] If we build robots with a psychology isomorphic with ours and a physical structure comparable to ours, should we award them civil rights? In contrast to Putnam, who thinks we can now give a more disinterested and hence objective answer to this question, I would say that our present answer, whatever it is, is so disinterested as to count for nothing. It seems to me that such questions about the robot or the fetus can't be answered in advance. This seems so for much the same reason that some things, especially regarding moral matters, can't be told to a child. A child can of course hear the words and operate with them, but he will not really understand them without undergoing certain experiences, and maybe not even then. Odd as it may sound, I want to know exactly what the robot looks like and what it's like to live with it. I want to know how in fact we—how I—look at it, respond to it, and feel toward it. Hypothetical situations of this sort raise questions which seem answerable only when the situation is realized, and perhaps then there is no longer a real question.

I am suggesting that what our natural response to a thing is, how we naturally react to it cognitively, affectively, and behaviorally, is partly definitive of that thing, and is therefore partly definitive of how we ought to respond to that thing. Often only an actual confrontation will tell us what we need to know, and sometimes we may each respond differently, and thus have differing understandings.

Moreover, the relation of such hypothetical situations to our actual situation is problematic. My hunch is that if the fetal condition I described were realized, fewer of us would be liberals and more of us would be conservatives and moderates. But suppose that in fact we would all be hidebound conservatives and that we knew that now. Would a contemporary liberal be irrational, unjustified, or wicked if he remained adamant? Well, if a slaveholder with a conscience were shown why he feels about Negroes as he does, and that he would regard them as his equals if only he had not been reared to think

18. "Robots: Machines or Artificially Created Life?" *The Journal of Philosophy* 61, no. 21 (1964): 668-691.

otherwise, he might change his ways, and if he didn't I would unhesitatingly call him irrational and his behavior unjustified and wicked.

But now suppose that dogs or chimps could and did talk, so that they entered our lives in more significant roles than those of experimental tools, friendly playthings, or faithful servants, and we enacted antivivisectionist legislation. If we discovered all this now, the news might deeply stir us, but would we necessarily be wrong if we still used animals as we do? Here, so I am inclined to think, we might sensibly maintain that in the hypothetical case the animals and their relations with us are essentially and relevantly different from what they now are. The capacities may exist now, but their realization constitutes a crucial change like that from an infant to an adult, and unlike that from a slave to a citizen. We would no more need to revise our treatment of animals than we need to apply the same principles of reciprocity to children and adults, a practice which, even if it weren't unfair, would be pointless and self-defeating—as resentful parents discover too late.

In the abortion case my instincts are similar but shakier. Yet I think that the adamant liberal could reply that what is special about fetuses, what distinguishes them from babies, slaves, animals, robots, and the rest, is that they essentially are and relate to us as bundles of potentialities. So, obviously, if their potentialities were actualized, not singly or partially, but in sufficient number and degree, we would feel differently. But to make them and their situation in respect to us different enough so that we would naturally regard them as human beings, they would have to become what they can become: human beings. In the hypothetical situation, they are babes in a biological incubator, and therefore that situation is irrelevant to our situation. In brief, an argument based on such a situation only restates the conservative's original argument with imaginary changes instead of the actual set of changes which transforms the fetus into a human child.

Does accepting the liberal's reply scotch all further argument? I think not. One obvious candidate for investigation is the principle that it is wrong to kill a human being, a principle to which some participants in the controversy, in particular utilitarians, apparently do not subscribe. Another candidate is the topic of euthanasia, which is part replica and part mirror image of the abortion problem: patients get described as vegetables, but their human status is elided because their capacities are exhausted rather than dormant. But such similarities may be only surface features; the substance of the two issues may lie in separate spaces. Either topic is as large and caliginous as that of abortion itself—discussable, but not here.

Instead, let me tempt you with a summary argument that the present abortion laws are illegitimate. The existence and powers of the state are legitimated through their rational acceptability to the citizenry, and it would be irrational for the citizens to grant the state any coercive power whose exercise *could* not be rationally justified to them. Thus, the state has the burden of proving that its actions are legitimate. Now, without question, the present abortion laws seriously restrict the freedom and diminish the welfare of the citizenry. A law with that effect is not *ipso facto* unjust, but the state has the burden of showing that such a law is necessary to attain the legitimate ends of the state. But the social costs of the present abortion laws are so drastic that only the preservation of human lives could justify them.[19] So to justify those laws the state must demonstrate that the fetus is a human being. But if that can't be done at all, the state can't do it either, so the laws must be deemed an unjustifiable burden and hence an illegitimate exercise of power.

Note carefully how limited this argument is. It does not show that abortions are morally okay; at best it shows that the legal prohibitions are not. Nor does it work against every possible prohibition of abortion; statutes having milder social liabilities might be warranted without arguing for the fetus' humanity. Further, while the laws are illegitimate because unjustifiable, they need not therefore be unjust; they might be just or unjust or neither without being demonstrably so. Finally, it does not follow that a conservative who promotes such prohibitions is reproachable.[20] What I said about the state does not apply to its citizens. If anything, the burden seems on the complaining liberals to show that a conservative is reprehensible when his political or personal behavior is unacceptable to the liberals. And while any

19. The truth of this claim may be arguable but becomes ever less so as the multiplication of mankind transforms the preservation of each new life into an increasingly direct threat to every human life.

20. The issue here was brought to my attention by Thomas Nagel.

constraint of liberty or any harm to others (e.g., an abortion law) is prima facie objectionable, so that the burden of proof is on its perpetrator, it is not evident that the perpetrator is criticizable when his victims are unsatisfied by an argument they cannot refute. So, for a citizen but not a state, to act without demonstrable justification is not to act wrongly.

MICHAEL TOOLEY Abortion and Infanticide[1]

This essay deals with the question of the morality of abortion and infanticide. The fundamental ethical objection traditionally advanced against these practices rests on the contention that human fetuses and infants have a right to life. It is this claim which will be the focus of attention here. The basic issue to be discussed, then, is what properties a thing must possess in order to have a serious right to life. My approach will be to set out and defend a basic moral principle specifying a condition an organism must satisfy if it is to have a serious right to life. It will be seen that this condition is not satisfied by human fetuses and infants, and thus that they do not have a right to life. So unless there are other substantial objections to abortion and infanticide, one is forced to conclude that these practices are morally acceptable ones. In contrast, it may turn out that our treatment of adult members of other species—cats, dogs, polar bears—is morally indefensible. For it is quite possible that such animals do possess properties that endow them with a right to life.

I. ABORTION AND INFANTICIDE

One reason the question of the morality of infanticide is worth examining is that it seems very difficult to formulate a completely satisfactory liberal position on abortion without coming to grips with the

1. I am grateful to a number of people, particularly the Editors of *Philosophy & Public Affairs*, Rodelia Hapke, and Walter Kaufmann, for their helpful comments. It should not, of course, be inferred that they share the views expressed in this paper.

infanticide issue. The problem the liberal encounters is essentially that of specifying a cutoff point which is not arbitrary: at what stage in the development of a human being does it cease to be morally permissible to destroy it? It is important to be clear about the difficulty here. The conservative's objection is not that since there is a continuous line of development from a zygote to a newborn baby, one must conclude that if it is seriously wrong to destroy a newborn baby it is also seriously wrong to destroy a zygote or any intermediate stage in the development of a human being. His point is rather that if one says it is wrong to destroy a newborn baby but not a zygote or some intermediate stage in the development of a human being, one should be prepared to point to a *morally relevant* difference between a newborn baby and the earlier stage in the development of a human being.

Precisely the same difficulty can, of course, be raised for a person who holds that infanticide is morally permissible. The conservative will ask what morally relevant differences there are between an adult human being and a newborn baby. What makes it morally permissible to destroy a baby, but wrong to kill an adult? So the challenge remains. But I will argue that in this case there is an extremely plausible answer.

Reflecting on the morality of infanticide forces one to face up to this challenge. In the case of abortion a number of events—quickening or viability, for instance—might be taken as cutoff points, and it is easy to overlook the fact that none of these events involves any morally significant change in the developing human. In contrast, if one is going to defend infanticide, one has to get very clear about what makes something a person, what gives something a right to life.

One of the interesting ways in which the abortion issue differs from most other moral issues is that the plausible positions on abortion appear to be extreme positions. For if a human fetus is a person, one is inclined to say that, in general, one would be justified in killing it only to save the life of the mother.[2] Such is the extreme conservative

2. Judith Jarvis Thomson (pp. 3-22) has argued with great force and ingenuity that this conclusion is mistaken. I will comment on her argument later.

position.[3] On the other hand, if the fetus is not a person, how can it be seriously wrong to destroy it? Why would one need to point to special circumstances to justify such action? The upshot is that there is no room for a moderate position on the issue of abortion such as one finds, for example, in the Model Penal Code recommendations.[4]

Aside from the light it may shed on the abortion question, the issue of infanticide is both interesting and important in its own right. The theoretical interest has been mentioned: it forces one to face up to the question of what makes something a person. The practical importance need not be labored. Most people would prefer to raise children who do not suffer from gross deformities or from severe physical, emotional, or intellectual handicaps. If it could be shown that there is no moral objection to infanticide the happiness of society could be significantly and justifiably increased.

Infanticide is also of interest because of the strong emotions it arouses. The typical reaction to infanticide is like the reaction to incest or cannibalism, or the reaction of previous generations to masturbation or oral sex. The response, rather than appealing to carefully formulated moral principles, is primarily visceral. When philosophers

3. While this is the position conservatives tend to hold, it is not clear that it is the position they ought to hold. For if the fetus is a person it is far from clear that it is permissible to destroy it to save the mother. Two moral principles lend support to the view that it is the fetus which should live. First, other things being equal, should not one give something to a person who has had less rather than to a person who has had more? The mother has had a chance to live, while the fetus has not. The choice is thus between giving the mother more of an opportunity to live while giving the fetus none at all and giving the fetus an opportunity to enjoy life while not giving the mother a further opportunity to do so. Surely fairness requires the latter. Secondly, since the fetus has a greater life expectancy than the mother, one is in effect distributing more goods by choosing the life of the fetus over the life of the mother.

The position I am here recommending to the conservative should not be confused with the official Catholic position. The Catholic Church holds that it is seriously wrong to kill a fetus directly even if failure to do so will result in the death of *both* the mother and the fetus. This perverse value judgment is not part of the conservative's position.

4. Section 230.3 of the American Law Institute's *Model Penal Code* (Philadelphia, 1962). There is some interesting, though at time confused, discussion of the proposed code in *Model Penal Code—Tentative Draft No. 9* (Philadelphia, 1959), pp. 146-162.

themselves respond in this way, offering no arguments, and dismissing infanticide out of hand, it is reasonable to suspect that one is dealing with a taboo rather than with a rational prohibition.[5] I shall attempt to show that this is in fact the case.

II. TERMINOLOGY: "PERSON" VERSUS "HUMAN BEING"

How is the term "person" to be interpreted? I shall treat the concept of a person as a purely moral concept, free of all descriptive content. Specifically, in my usage the sentence "X is a person" will be synonymous with the sentence "X has a (serious) moral right to life."

This usage diverges slightly from what is perhaps the more common way of interpreting the term "person" when it is employed as a purely moral term, where to say that X is a person is to say that X has rights. If everything that had rights had a right to life, these interpretations would be extensionally equivalent. But I am inclined to think that it does not follow from acceptable moral principles that whatever has any rights at all has a right to life. My reason is this. Given the choice between being killed and being tortured for an hour, most adult humans would surely choose the latter. So it seems plausible to say it is worse to kill an adult human being than it is to torture him for an hour. In contrast, it seems to me that while it is not seriously wrong to kill a newborn kitten, it is seriously wrong to torture one for an hour. This *suggests* that newborn kittens may have a right not to be tortured without having a serious right to life. For it seems to be true that an individual has a right to something whenever it is the case that, if he wants that thing, it would be wrong for others to deprive him of it. Then if it is wrong to inflict a certain sensation upon a kitten if it doesn't want to experience that sensation, it will follow that the kitten has a right not to have sensation inflicted upon it.[6] I shall re-

5. A clear example of such an unwillingness to entertain seriously the possibility that moral judgments widely accepted in one's own society may nevertheless be incorrect is provided by Roger Wertheimer's superficial dismissal of infanticide on pages 25-26.

6. Compare the discussion of the concept of a right offered by Richard B. Brandt in his *Ethical Theory* (Englewood Cliffs, N.J., 1959), pp. 434-441. As Brandt points out, some philosophers have maintained that only things that can *claim* rights can have rights. I agree with Brandt's view that "inability to claim does not destroy the right" (p. 440).

turn to this example later. My point here is merely that it provides some reason for holding that it does not follow from acceptable moral principles that if something has any rights at all, it has a serious right to life.

There has been a tendency in recent discussions of abortion to use expressions such as "person" and "human being" interchangeably. B. A. Brody, for example, refers to the difficulty of determining "whether destroying the foetus constitutes the taking of a human life," and suggests it is very plausible that "the taking of a human life is an action that has bad consequences for him whose life is being taken."[7] When Brody refers to something as a human life he apparently construes this as entailing that the thing is a person. For if every living organism belonging to the species homo sapiens counted as a human life, there would be no difficulty in determining whether a fetus inside a human mother was a human life.

The same tendency is found in Judith Jarvis Thomson's article, which opens with the statement: "Most opposition to abortion relies on the premise that the fetus is a human being, a person, from the moment of conception."[8] The same is true of Roger Wertheimer, who explicitly says: "First off I should note that the expressions 'a human life,' 'a human being,' 'a person' are virtually interchangeable in this context."[9]

The tendency to use expressions like "person" and "human being" interchangeably is an unfortunate one. For one thing, it tends to lend covert support to antiabortionist positions. Given such usage, one who holds a liberal view of abortion is put in the position of maintaining that fetuses, at least up to a certain point, are not human beings. Even philosophers are led astray by this usage. Thus Wertheimer says that "except for monstrosities, every member of our species is indubitably a person, a human being, at the very latest at birth."[10] Is it really *indubitable* that newborn babies are persons? Surely this is a wild contention. Wertheimer is falling prey to the confusion naturally

7. B. A. Brody, "Abortion and the Law," *Journal of Philosophy*, LXVIII, no. 12 (17 June 1971): 357-369. See pp. 357-358.

8. P. 3.

9. P. 25.

10. *Ibid.*

engendered by the practice of using "person" and "human being" inter-changeably. Another example of this is provided by Thomson: "I am inclined to think also that we shall probably have to agree that the fetus has already become a human person well before birth. Indeed, it comes as a surprise when one first learns how early in its life it be-gins to acquire human characteristics. By the tenth week, for example, it already has a face, arms and legs, fingers and toes; it has internal organs, and brain activity is detectable."[11] But what do such physio-logical characteristics have to do with the question of whether the organism is a person? Thomson, partly, I think, because of the un-fortunate use of terminology, does not even raise this question. As a result she virtually takes it for granted that there are some cases in which abortion is "positively indecent."[12]

There is a second reason why using "person" and "human being" interchangeably is unhappy philosophically. If one says that the dis-pute between pro- and anti-abortionists centers on whether the fetus is a human, it is natural to conclude that it is essentially a disagree-ment about certain facts, a disagreement about what properties a fetus possesses. Thus Wertheimer says that "if one insists on using the raggy fact-value distinction, then one ought to say that the dispute is over a matter of fact in the sense in which it is a fact that the Negro slaves were human beings."[13] I shall argue that the two cases are not parallel, and that in the case of abortion what is primarily at stake is what moral principles one should accept. If one says that the central issue between conservatives and liberals in the abortion ques-tion is whether the fetus is a person, it is clear that the dispute may be either about what properties a thing must have in order to be a person, in order to have a right to life—a moral question—or about whether a fetus at a given stage of development as a matter of fact possesses the properties in question. The temptation to suppose that the disagree-ment must be a factual one is removed.

It should now be clear why the common practice of using expres-sions such as "person" and "human being" interchangeably in dis-cussions of abortion is unfortunate. It would perhaps be best to avoid

11. Pp. 3-4.
12. P. 21.
13. P. 34.

the term "human" altogether, employing instead some expression that is more naturally interpreted as referring to a certain type of biological organism characterized in physiological terms, such as "member of the species Homo sapiens." My own approach will be to use the term "human" only in contexts where it is not philosophically dangerous.

III. THE BASIC ISSUE: WHEN IS A MEMBER OF THE SPECIES HOMO SAPIENS A PERSON?

Settling the issue of the morality of abortion and infanticide will involve answering the following questions: What properties must something have to be a person, i.e., to have a serious right to life? At what point in the development of a member of the species Homo sapiens does the organism possess the properties that make it a person? The first question raises a moral issue. To answer it is to decide what basic[14] moral principles involving the ascription of a right to life one ought to accept. The second question raises a purely factual issue, since the properties in question are properties of a purely descriptive sort.

Some writers seem quite pessimistic about the possibility of resolving the question of the morality of abortion. Indeed, some have gone so far as to suggest that the question of whether the fetus is a person is in principle unanswerable: "we seem to be stuck with the indeterminateness of the fetus' humanity."[15] An understanding of some of the sources of this pessimism will, I think, help us to tackle the problem. Let us begin by considering the similarity a number of people have noted between the issue of abortion and the issue of Negro slavery. The question here is why it should be more difficult to decide whether abortion and infanticide are acceptable than it was to decide whether slavery was acceptable. The answer seems to be that in the case of slavery there are moral principles of a quite uncontroversial sort that settle the issue. Thus most people would agree to some such principle as the following: No organism that has experiences, that is capable of thought and of using language, and that has harmed no one, should

14. A moral principle accepted by a person is *basic for him* if and only if his acceptance of it is not dependent upon any of his (nonmoral) factual beliefs. That is, no change in his factual beliefs would cause him to abandon the principle in question.

15. Wertheimer, p. 44.

be made a slave. In the case of abortion, on the other hand, conditions that are generally agreed to be sufficient grounds for ascribing a right to life to something do not suffice to settle the issue. It is easy to specify other, purportedly sufficient conditions that will settle the issue, but no one has been successful in putting forward considerations that will convince others to accept those additional moral principles.

I do not share the general pessimism about the possibility of resolving the issue of abortion and infanticide because I believe it is possible to point to a very plausible moral principle dealing with the question of *necessary* conditions for something's having a right to life, where the conditions in question will provide an answer to the question of the permissibility of abortion and infanticide.

There is a second cause of pessimism that should be noted before proceeding. It is tied up with the fact that the development of an organism is one of gradual and continuous change. Given this continuity, how is one to draw a line at one point and declare it permissible to destroy a member of Homo sapiens up to, but not beyond, that point? Won't there be an arbitrariness about any point that is chosen? I will return to this worry shortly. It does not present a serious difficulty once the basic moral principles relevant to the ascription of a right to life to an individual are established.

Let us turn now to the first and most fundamental question: What properties must something have in order to be a person, i.e., to have a serious right to life? The claim I wish to defend is this: An organism possesses a serious right to life only if it possesses the concept of a self as a continuing subject of experiences and other mental states, and believes that it is itself such a continuing entity.

My basic argument in support of this claim, which I will call the self-consciousness requirement, will be clearest, I think, if I first offer a simplified version of the argument, and then consider a modification that seems desirable. The simplified version of my argument is this. To ascribe a right to an individual is to assert something about the prima facie obligations of other individuals to act, or to refrain from acting, in certain ways. However, the obligations in question are conditional ones, being dependent upon the existence of certain desires of the individual to whom the right is ascribed. Thus if an individual asks one to destroy something to which he has a right, one does not violate his right to that thing if one proceeds to destroy it. This sug-. gests the following analysis: "A has a right to X" is roughly synonymous with "If A desires X, then others are under a prima facie obligation to refrain from actions that would deprive him of it."[16]

Although this analysis is initially plausible, there are reasons for thinking it not entirely correct. I will consider these later. Even here, however, some expansion is necessary, since there are features of the concept of a right that are important in the present context, and that ought to be dealt with more explicitly. In particular, it seems to be a conceptual truth that things that lack consciousness, such as ordinary machines, cannot have rights. Does this conceptual truth follow from the above analysis of the concept of a right? The answer depends on how the term "desire" is interpreted. If one adopts a completely behavioristic interpretation of "desire," so that a machine that searches for an electrical outlet in order to get its batteries recharged is described as having a desire to be recharged, then it will not follow from this analysis that objects that lack consciousness cannot have rights. On the other hand, if "desire" is interpreted in such a way that desires are states necessarily standing in some sort of relationship to states of consciousness, it will follow from the analysis that a machine that is not capable of being conscious, and consequently of having desires, cannot have any rights. I think those who defend analyses of the concept of a right along the lines of this one do have in mind an interpretation of the term "desire" that involves reference to something more than behavioral dispositions. However, rather than relying on this, it seems preferable to make such an interpretation explicit. The following analysis is a natural way of doing that: "A has a right to X" is roughly synonymous with "A is the sort of thing that is a subject of experiences and other mental states, A is capable of desiring X, and if A does desire X, then others are under a prima facie obligation to refrain from actions that would deprive him of it."

The next step in the argument is basically a matter of applying this analysis to the concept of a right to life. Unfortunately the expression

16. Again, compare the analysis defended by Brandt in *Ethical Theory*, pp. 434-441.

"right to life" is not entirely a happy one, since it suggests that the right in question concerns the continued existence of a biological organism. That this is incorrect can be brought out by considering possible ways of violating an individual's right to life. Suppose, for example, that by some technology of the future the brain of an adult human were to be completely reprogrammed, so that the organism wound up with memories (or rather, apparent memories), beliefs, attitudes, and personality traits completely different from those associated with it before it was subjected to reprogramming. In such a case one would surely say that an individual had been destroyed, that an adult human's right to life had been violated, even though no biological organism had been killed. This example shows that the expression "right to life" is misleading, since what one is really concerned about is not just the continued existence of a biological organism, but the right of a subject of experiences and other mental states to continue to exist.

Given this more precise description of the right with which we are here concerned, we are now in a position to apply the analysis of the concept of a right stated above. When we do so we find that the statement "A has a right to continue to exist as a subject of experiences and other mental states" is roughly synonymous with the statement "A is a subject of experiences and other mental states, A is capable of desiring to continue to exist as a subject of experiences and other mental states, and if A does desire to continue to exist as such an entity, then others are under a prima facie obligation not to prevent him from doing so."

The final stage in the argument is simply a matter of asking what must be the case if something is to be capable of having a desire to continue existing as a subject of experiences and other mental states. The basic point here is that the desires a thing can have are limited by the concepts it possesses. For the fundamental way of describing a given desire is as a desire that a certain proposition be true.[17] Then,

17. In everyday life one often speaks of desiring things, such as an apple or a newspaper. Such talk is elliptical, the context together with one's ordinary beliefs serving to make it clear that one wants to eat the apple and read the newspaper. To say that what one desires is that a certain proposition be true should not be construed as involving any particular ontological commitment. The point is merely that it is sentences such as "John wants it to be the case

since one cannot desire that a certain proposition be true unless one understands it, and since one cannot understand it without possessing the concepts involved in it, it follows that the desires one can have are limited by the concepts one possesses. Applying this to the present case results in the conclusion that an entity cannot be the sort of thing that can desire that a subject of experiences and other mental states exist unless it possesses the concept of such a subject. Moreover, an entity cannot desire that it itself *continue* existing as a subject of experiences and other mental states unless it believes that it is now such a subject. This completes the justification of the claim that it is a necessary condition of something's having a serious right to life that it possess the concept of a self as a continuing subject of experiences, and that it believe that it is itself such an entity.

Let us now consider a modification in the above argument that seems desirable. This modification concerns the crucial conceptual claim advanced about the relationship between ascription of rights and ascription of the corresponding desires. Certain situations suggest that there may be exceptions to the claim that if a person doesn't desire something, one cannot violate his right to it. There are three types of situations that call this claim into question: (i) situations in which an individual's desires reflect a state of emotional disturbance; (ii) situations in which a previously conscious individual is temporarily unconscious; (iii) situations in which an individual's desires have been distorted by conditioning or by indoctrination.

As an example of the first, consider a case in which an adult human falls into a state of depression which his psychiatrist recognizes as temporary. While in the state he tells people he wishes he were dead. His psychiatrist, accepting the view that there can be no violation of an individual's right to life unless the individual has a desire to live, decides to let his patient have his way and kills him. Or consider a related case in which one person gives another a drug that produces a state of temporary depression; the recipient expresses a wish that he were dead. The person who administered the drug then kills him. Doesn't one want to say in both these cases that the agent did some-

that he is eating an apple in the next few minutes" that provide a completely explicit description of a person's desires. If one fails to use such sentences one can be badly misled about what concepts are presupposed by a particular desire.

thing seriously wrong in killing the other person? And isn't the reason the action was seriously wrong in each case the fact that it violated the individual's right to life? If so, the right to life cannot be linked with a desire to live in the way claimed above.

The second set of situations are ones in which an individual is unconscious for some reason—that is, he is sleeping, or drugged, or in a temporary coma. Does an individual in such a state have any desires? People do sometimes say that an unconscious individual wants something, but it might be argued that if such talk is not to be simply false it must be interpreted as actually referring to the desires the individual *would* have if he were now conscious. Consequently, if the analysis of the concept of a right proposed above were correct, it would follow that one does not violate an individual's right if one takes his car, or kills him, while he is asleep.

Finally, consider situations in which an individual's desires have been distorted, either by inculcation of irrational beliefs or by direct conditioning. Thus an individual may permit someone to kill him because he has been convinced that if he allows himself to be sacrificed to the gods he will be gloriously rewarded in a life to come. Or an individual may be enslaved after first having been conditioned to desire a life of slavery. Doesn't one want to say that in the former case an individual's right to life has been violated, and in the latter his right to freedom?

Situations such as these strongly suggest that even if an individual doesn't want something, it is still possible to violate his right to it. Some modification of the earlier account of the concept of a right thus seems in order. The analysis given covers, I believe, the paradigmatic cases of violation of an individual's rights, but there are other, secondary cases where one also wants to say that someone's right has been violated which are not included.

Precisely how the revised analysis should be formulated is unclear. Here it will be sufficient merely to say that, in view of the above, an individual's right to X can be violated not only when he desires X, but also when he *would* now desire X were it not for one of the following: (i) he is in an emotionally unbalanced state; (ii) he is temporarily unconscious; (iii) he has been conditioned to desire the absence of X.

The critical point now is that, even given this extension of the conditions under which an individual's right to something can be violated, it is still true that one's right to something can be violated only when one has the conceptual capability of desiring the thing in question. For example, an individual who would now desire not to be a slave if he weren't emotionally unbalanced, or if he weren't temporarily unconscious, or if he hadn't previously been conditioned to want to be a slave, must possess the concepts involved in the desire not to be a slave. Since it is really only the conceptual capability presupposed by the desire to continue existing as a subject of experiences and other mental states, and not the desire itself, that enters into the above argument, the modification required in the account of the conditions under which an individual's rights can be violated does not undercut my defense of the self-consciousness requirement.[18]

To sum up, my argument has been that having a right to life presupposes that one is capable of desiring to continue existing as a subject of experiences and other mental states. This in turn presupposes both that one has the concept of such a continuing entity and that one believes that one is oneself such an entity. So an entity that lacks such a consciousness of itself as a continuing subject of mental states does not have a right to life.

It would be natural to ask at this point whether satisfaction of this requirement is not only necessary but also sufficient to ensure that a thing has a right to life. I am inclined to an affirmative answer. However, the issue is not urgent in the present context, since as long as the requirement is in fact a necessary one we have the basis of an adequate defense of abortion and infanticide. If an organism must satisfy some other condition before it has a serious right to life, the result

18. There are, however, situations other than those discussed here which might seem to count against the claim that a person cannot have a right unless he is conceptually capable of having the corresponding desire. Can't a young child, for example, have a right to an estate, even though he may not be conceptually capable of wanting the estate? It is clear that such situations have to be carefully considered if one is to arrive at a satisfactory account of the concept of a right. My inclination is to say that the correct description is not that the child now has a right to the estate, but that he will come to have such a right when he is mature, and that in the meantime no one else has a right to the estate. My reason for saying that the child does not now have a right to the estate is that he cannot now do things with the estate, such as selling it or giving it away, that he will be able to do later on.

will merely be that the interval during which infanticide is morally permissible may be somewhat longer. Although the point at which an organism first achieves self-consciousness and hence the capacity of desiring to continue existing as a subject of experiences and other mental states may be a theoretically incorrect cutoff point, it is at least a morally safe one: any error it involves is on the side of caution.

IV. SOME CRITICAL COMMENTS ON ALTERNATIVE PROPOSALS

I now want to compare the line of demarcation I am proposing with the cutoff points traditionally advanced in discussions of abortion. My fundamental claim will be that none of these cutoff points can be defended by appeal to plausible, basic moral principles. The main suggestions as to the point past which it is seriously wrong to destroy something that will develop into an adult member of the species Homo sapiens are these: (a) conception; (b) the attainment of human form; (c) the achievement of the ability to move about spontaneously; (d) viability; (e) birth.[19] The corresponding moral principles suggested by these cutoff points are as follows: (1) It is seriously wrong to kill an organism, from a zygote on, that belongs to the species Homo sapiens. (2) It is seriously wrong to kill an organism that belongs to Homo sapiens and that has achieved human form. (3) It is seriously wrong to kill an organism that is a member of Homo sapiens and that is capable of spontaneous movement. (4) It is seriously wrong to kill an organism that belongs to Homo sapiens and that is capable of existing outside the womb. (5) It is seriously wrong to kill an organism that is a member of Homo sapiens that is no longer in the womb.

My first comment is that it would not do *simply* to omit the reference to membership in the species Homo sapiens from the above principles, with the exception of principle (2). For then the principles would be applicable to animals in general, and one would be forced to conclude that it was seriously wrong to abort a cat fetus, or that it was seriously wrong to abort a motile cat fetus, and so on.

The second and crucial comment is that none of the five principles

19. Another frequent suggestion as to the cutoff point not listed here is quickening. I omit it because it seems clear that if abortion after quickening is wrong, its wrongness must be tied up with the motility of the fetus, not with the mother's awareness of the fetus' ability to move about.

given above can plausibly be viewed as a *basic* moral principle. To accept any of them as such would be akin to accepting as a basic moral principle the proposition that it is morally permissible to enslave black members of the species Homo sapiens but not white members. Why should it be seriously wrong to kill an unborn member of the species Homo sapiens but not seriously wrong to kill an unborn kitten? Difference in species is not per se a morally relevant difference. If one holds that it is seriously wrong to kill an unborn member of the species Homo sapiens but not an unborn kitten, one should be prepared to point to some property that is morally significant and that is possessed by unborn members of Homo sapiens but not by unborn kittens. Similarly, such a property must be identified if one believes it seriously wrong to kill unborn members of Homo sapiens that have achieved viability but not seriously wrong to kill unborn kittens that have achieved that state.

What property might account for such a difference? That is to say, what *basic* moral principles might a person who accepts one of these five principles appeal to in support of his secondary moral judgment? Why should events such as the achievement of human form, or the achievement of the ability to move about, or the achievement of viability, or birth serve to endow something with a right to life? What the liberal must do is to show that these events involve changes, or are associated with changes, that are morally relevant.

Let us now consider reasons why the events involved in cutoff points (b) through (e) are not morally relevant, beginning with the last two: viability and birth. The fact that an organism is not physiologically dependent upon another organism, or is capable of such physiological independence, is surely irrelevant to whether the organism has a right to life. In defense of this contention, consider a speculative case where a fetus is able to learn a language while in the womb. One would surely not say that the fetus had no right to life until it emerged from the womb, or until it was capable of existing outside the womb. A less speculative example is the case of Siamese twins who have learned to speak. One doesn't want to say that since one of the twins would die were the two to be separated, it therefore has no right to life. Consequently it seems difficult to disagree with the conservative's claim that an organism which lacks a right to life before birth or before becoming viable cannot acquire this right immediately upon birth or upon becoming viable.

This does not, however, completely rule out viability as a line of demarcation. For instead of defending viability as a cutoff point on the ground that only then does a fetus acquire a right to life, it is possible to argue rather that when one organism is physiologically dependent upon another, the former's right to life may conflict with the latter's right to use its body as it will, and moreover, that the latter's right to do what it wants with its body may often take precedence over the other organism's right to life. Thomson has defended this view: "I am arguing only that having a right to life does not guarantee having either a right to the use of or a right to be allowed continued use of another person's body—even if one needs it for life itself. So the right to life will not serve the opponents of abortion in the very simple and clear way in which they seem to have thought it would."[20] I believe that Thomson is right in contending that philosophers have been altogether too casual in assuming that if one grants the fetus a serious right to life, one must accept a conservative position on abortion.[21] I also think the only defense of viability as a cutoff point which has any hope of success at all is one based on the considerations she advances. I doubt very much, however, that this defense of abortion is ultimately tenable. I think that one can grant even stronger assumptions than those made by Thomson and still argue persuasively for a semiconservative view. What I have in mind is this. Let it be granted, for the sake of argument, that a woman's right to free her body of parasites which will inhibit her freedom of action and possibly impair her health is stronger than the parasite's right to life, and is so even if the parasite has as much right to life as an adult human. One can still argue that abortion ought not to be permitted. For if A's right is stronger than B's, and it is impossible to satisfy both, it does not follow that A's should be satisfied rather than B's. It may be possible to compensate A if his right isn't satisfied, but impossible to compensate B if his right isn't satisfied. In such a case the best thing

20. P. 12.
21. A good example of a failure to probe this issue is provided by Brody's "Abortion and the Law."

to do may be to satisfy B's claim and to compensate A. Abortion may be a case in point. If the fetus has a right to life and the right is not satisfied, there is certainly no way the fetus can be compensated. On the other hand, if the woman's right to rid her body of harmful and annoying parasites is not satisfied, she can be compensated. Thus it would seem that the just thing to do would be to prohibit abortion, but to compensate women for the burden of carrying a parasite to term. Then, however, we are back at a (modified) conservative position.[22] Our conclusion must be that it appears unlikely there is any satisfactory defense either of viability or of birth as cutoff points.

Let us now consider the third suggested line of demarcation, the achievement of the power to move about spontaneously. It might be argued that acquiring this power is a morally relevant event on the grounds that there is a connection between the concept of an agent and the concept of a person, and being motile is an indication that a thing is an agent.[23]

It is difficult to respond to this suggestion unless it is made more specific. Given that one's interest here is in defending a certain cutoff point, it is natural to interpret the proposal as suggesting that motility is a necessary condition of an organism's having a right to life. But this won't do, because one certainly wants to ascribe a right to life to adult humans who are completely paralyzed. Maybe the suggestion is rather that motility is a sufficient condition of something's having a right to life. However, it is clear that motility alone is not sufficient, since this would imply that all animals, and also certain machines, have a right to life. Perhaps, then, the most reasonable interpretation of the claim is that motility together with some other property is a sufficient condition of something's having a right to life, where the other property will have to be a property possessed by unborn members of the species Homo sapiens but not by unborn members of other familiar species.

The central question, then, is what this other property is. Until one

22. Admittedly the modification is a substantial one, since given a society that refused to compensate women, a woman who had an abortion would not be doing anything wrong.

23. Compare Wertheimer's remarks, p. 35.

is told, it is very difficult to evaluate either the moral claim that motility together with that property is a sufficient basis for ascribing to an organism a right to life or the factual claim that a motile human fetus possesses that property while a motile fetus belonging to some other species does not. A conservative would presumably reject motility as a cutoff point by arguing that whether an organism has a right to life depends only upon its potentialities, which are of course not changed by its becoming motile. If, on the other hand, one favors a liberal view of abortion, I think that one can attack this third suggested cutoff point, in its unspecified form, only by determining what properties are necessary, or what properties sufficient, for an individual to have a right to life. Thus I would base my rejection of motility as a cutoff point on my claim, defended above, that a necessary condition of an organism's possessing a right to life is that it conceive of itself as a continuing subject of experiences and other mental states.

The second suggested cutoff point—the development of a recognizably human form—can be dismissed fairly quickly. I have already remarked that membership in a particular species is not itself a morally relevant property. For it is obvious that if we encountered other "rational animals," such as Martians, the fact that their physiological makeup was very different from our own would not be grounds for denying them a right to life.[24] Similarly, it is clear that the development of human form is not in itself a morally relevant event. Nor do there seem to be any grounds for holding that there is some other change, associated with this event, that is morally relevant. The appeal of this second cutoff point is, I think, purely emotional.

The overall conclusion seems to be that it is very difficult to defend the cutoff points traditionally advanced by those who advocate either a moderate or a liberal position on abortion. The reason is that there do not seem to be any basic moral principles one can appeal to in support of the cutoff points in question. We must now consider whether the conservative is any better off.

24. This requires qualification. If their central nervous systems were radically different from ours, it might be thought that one would not be justified in ascribing to them mental states of an experiential sort. And then, since it seems to be a conceptual truth that only things having experiential states can have rights, one would be forced to conclude that one was not justified in ascribing any rights to them.

V. REFUTATION OF THE CONSERVATIVE POSITION

Many have felt that the conservative's position is more defensible than the liberal's because the conservative can point to the gradual and continuous development of an organism as it changes from a zygote to an adult human being. He is then in a position to argue that it is morally arbitrary for the liberal to draw a line at some point in this continuous process and to say that abortion is permissible before, but not after, that particular point. The liberal's reply would presumably be that the emphasis upon the continuity of the process is misleading. What the conservative is really doing is simply challenging the liberal to specify the properties a thing must have in order to be a person, and to show that the developing organism does acquire the properties at the point selected by the liberal. The liberal may then reply that the difficulty he has meeting this challenge should not be taken as grounds for rejecting his position. For the conservative cannot meet this challenge either; the conservative is equally unable to say what properties something must have if it is to have a right to life.

Although this rejoinder does not dispose of the conservative's argument, it is not without bite. For defenders of the view that abortion is always wrong have failed to face up to the question of the basic moral principles on which their position rests. They have been content to assert the wrongness of killing any organism, from a zygote on, if that organism is a member of the species Homo sapiens. But they have overlooked the point that this cannot be an acceptable *basic* moral principle, since difference in species is not in itself a morally relevant difference. The conservative can reply, however, that it is possible to defend his position—but not the liberal's—*without* getting clear about the properties a thing must possess if it is to have a right to life. The conservative's defense will rest upon the following two claims: first, that there is a property, even if one is unable to specify what it is, that (i) is possessed by adult humans, and (ii) endows any organism possessing it with a serious right to life. Second, that if there are properties which satisfy (i) and (ii) above, at least one of those properties will be such that any organism potentially possessing that property has a serious right to life even now, simply by virtue of that potentiality, where an organism possesses a property potentially if it will come to have that property in the normal course of its development. The second claim—which I shall refer to as the potentiality principle—is critical to the conservative's defense. Because of it he is able to defend his position without deciding what properties a thing must possess in order to have a right to life. It is enough to know that adult members of Homo sapiens do have such a right. For then one can conclude that any organism which belongs to the species Homo sapiens, from a zygote on, must also have a right to life by virtue of the potentiality principle.

The liberal, by contrast, cannot mount a comparable argument. He cannot defend his position without offering at least a partial answer to the question of what properties a thing must possess in order to have a right to life.

The importance of the potentiality principle, however, goes beyond the fact that it provides support for the conservative's position. If the principle is unacceptable, then so is his position. For if the conservative cannot defend the view that an organism's having certain potentialities is sufficient grounds for ascribing to it a right to life, his claim that a fetus which is a member of Homo sapiens has a right to life can be attacked as follows. The reason an adult member of Homo sapiens has a right to life, but an infant ape does not, is that there are certain psychological properties which the former possesses and the latter lacks. Now, even if one is unsure exactly what these psychological properties are, it is clear that an organism in the early stages of development from a zygote into an adult member of Homo sapiens does not possess these properties. One need merely compare a human fetus with an ape fetus. What mental states does the former enjoy that the latter does not? Surely it is reasonable to hold that there are no significant differences in their respective mental lives—assuming that one wishes to ascribe any mental states at all to such organisms. (Does a zygote have a mental life? Does it have experiences? Or beliefs? Or desires?) There are, of course, physiological differences, but these are not in themselves morally significant. *If* one held that potentialities were relevant to the ascription of a right to life, one could argue that the physiological differences, though not morally significant in themselves, are morally significant by virtue of their causal consequences: they will lead to later psychological differences that are morally relevant, and for this reason the physiological differences are themselves morally significant. But if the potentiality principle is not available, this line of argument cannot be used, and there will then be no differences between a human fetus and an ape fetus that the conservative can use as grounds for ascribing a serious right to life to the former but not to the latter.

It is therefore tempting to conclude that the conservative view of abortion is acceptable if and only if the potentiality principle is acceptable. But to say that the conservative position can be defended if the potentiality principle is acceptable is to assume that the argument is over once it is granted that the fetus has a right to life, and, as was noted above, Thomson has shown that there are serious grounds for questioning this assumption. In any case, the important point here is that the conservative position on abortion is acceptable *only if* the potentiality principle is sound.

One way to attack the potentiality principle is simply to argue in support of the self-consciousness requirement—the claim that only an organism that conceives of itself as a continuing subject of experiences has a right to life. For this requirement, when taken together with the claim that there is at least one property, possessed by adult humans, such that any organism possessing it has a serious right to life, entails the denial of the potentiality principle. Or at least this is so if we add the uncontroversial empirical claim that an organism that will in the normal course of events develop into an adult human does not from the very beginning of its existence possess a concept of a continuing subject of experiences together with a belief that it is itself such an entity.

I think it best, however, to scrutinize the potentiality principle itself, and not to base one's case against it simply on the self-consciousness requirement. Perhaps the first point to note is that the potentiality principle should not be confused with principles such as the following: the value of an object is related to the value of the things into which it can develop. This "valuation principle" is rather vague. There are ways of making it more precise, but we need not consider these here. Suppose now that one were to speak not of a right to life, but of the value of life. It would then be easy to make the mistake of thinking that the valuation principle was relevant to the potentiality principle—indeed, that it entailed it. But an individual's right to life is not based on the value of his life. To say that the world would be better off if it contained fewer people is not to say that it would be right to achieve such a better world by killing some of the present inhabitants. *If* having a right to life were a matter of a thing's value, then a thing's potentialities, being connected with its expected value, would clearly be relevant to the question of what rights it had. Conversely, once one realizes that a thing's rights are not a matter of its value, I think it becomes clear that an organism's potentialities are irrelevant to the question of whether it has a right to life.

But let us now turn to the task of finding a direct refutation of the potentiality principle. The basic issue is this. Is there any property J which satisfies the following conditions: (1) There is a property K such that any individual possessing property K has a right to life, and there is a scientific law L to the effect that any organism possessing property J will in the normal course of events come to possess property K at some later time. (2) Given the relationship between property J and property K just described, anything possessing property J has a right to life. (3) If property J were not related to property K in the way indicated, it would not be the case that anything possessing property J thereby had a right to life. In short, the question is whether there is a property J that bestows a right to life on an organism *only because* J stands in a certain causal relationship to a second property K, which is such that anything possessing that property ipso facto has a right to life.

My argument turns upon the following critical principle: Let C be a causal process that normally leads to outcome E. Let A be an action that initiates process C, and B be an action involving a minimal expenditure of energy that stops process C before outcome E occurs. Assume further that actions A and B do not have any other consequences, and that E is the only morally significant outcome of process C. Then there is no moral difference between intentionally performing action B and intentionally refraining from performing action A, assuming identical motivation in both cases. This principle, which I shall refer to as the moral symmetry principle with respect to action and inaction, would be rejected by some philosophers. They would argue that there is an important distinction to be drawn between "what we owe people in the form of aid and what we owe them in the way of non-interference,"[25] and that the latter, "negative duties," are duties that it is more serious to neglect than the former, "positive" ones. This view arises from an intuitive response to examples such as the following. Even if it is wrong not to send food to starving people in other parts of the world, it is more wrong still to kill someone. And isn't the conclusion, then, that one's obligation to refrain from killing someone is a more serious obligation than one's obligation to save lives?

I want to argue that this is not the correct conclusion. I think it is tempting to draw this conclusion if one fails to consider the motivation that is likely to be associated with the respective actions. If someone performs an action he knows will kill someone else, this will usually be grounds for concluding that he wanted to kill the person in question. In contrast, failing to help someone may indicate only apathy, laziness, selfishness, or an amoral outlook: the fact that a person knowingly allows another to die will not normally be grounds for concluding that he desired that person's death. Someone who knowingly kills another is more likely to be seriously defective from a moral point of view than someone who fails to save another's life.

If we are not to be led to false conclusions by our intuitions about certain cases, we must explicitly assume identical motivations in the two situations. Compare, for example, the following: (1) Jones sees that Smith will be killed by a bomb unless he warns him. Jones's reaction is: "How lucky, it will save me the trouble of killing Smith myself." So Jones allows Smith to be killed by the bomb, even though he could easily have warned him. (2) Jones wants Smith dead, and therefore shoots him. Is one to say there is a significant difference between the wrongness of Jones's behavior in these two cases? Surely not. This shows the mistake of drawing a distinction between positive duties and negative duties and holding that the latter impose stricter obligations than the former. The difference in our intuitions about situations that involve giving aid to others and corresponding situations that involve not interfering with others is to be explained by reference to probable differences in the motivations operating in the

25. Philippa Foot, "The Problem of Abortion and the Doctrine of the Double Effect," *The Oxford Review* 5 (1967): 5-15. See the discussion on pp. 11ff.

two situations, and not by reference to a distinction between positive and negative duties. For once it is specified that the motivation is the same in the two situations, we realize that inaction is as wrong in the one case as action is in the other.

There is another point that may be relevant. Action involves effort, while inaction usually does not. It usually does not require any effort on my part to refrain from killing someone, but saving someone's life will require an expenditure of energy. One must then ask how large a sacrifice a person is morally required to make to save the life of another. If the sacrifice of time and energy is quite large it may be that one is not morally obliged to save the life of another in that situation. Superficial reflection upon such cases might easily lead us to introduce the distinction between positive and negative duties, but again it is clear that this would be a mistake. The point is not that one has a greater duty to refrain from killing others than to perform positive actions that will save them. It is rather that positive actions require effort, and this means that in deciding what to do a person has to take into account his own right to do what he wants with his life, and not only the other person's right to life. To avoid this confusion, we should confine ourselves to comparisons between situations in which the positive action involves minimal effort.

The moral symmetry principle, as formulated above, explicitly takes these two factors into account. It applies only to pairs of situations in which the motivations are identical and the positive action involves minimal effort. Without these restrictions, the principle would be open to serious objection; with them, it seems perfectly acceptable. For the central objection to it rests on the claim that we must distinguish positive from negative duties and recognize that negative duties impose stronger obligations than positive ones. I have tried to show how this claim derives from an unsound account of our moral intuitions about certain situations.

My argument against the potentiality principle can now be stated. Suppose at some future time a chemical were to be discovered which when injected into the brain of a kitten would cause the kitten to develop into a cat possessing a brain of the sort possessed by humans, and consequently into a cat having all the psychological capabilities characteristic of adult humans. Such cats would be able to think, to use language, and so on. Now it would surely be morally indefensible in such a situation to ascribe a serious right to life to members of the species Homo sapiens without also ascribing it to cats that have undergone such a process of development: there would be no morally significant differences.

Secondly, it would not be seriously wrong to refain from injecting a newborn kitten with the special chemical, and to kill it instead. The fact that one could initiate a causal process that would transform a kitten into an entity that would eventually possess properties such that anything possessing them ipso facto has a serious right to life does not mean that the kitten has a serious right to life even before it has been subjected to the process of injection and transformation. The possibility of transforming kittens into persons will not make it any more wrong to kill newborn kittens than it is now.

Thirdly, in view of the symmetry principle, if it is not seriously wrong to refrain from initiating such a causal process, neither is it seriously wrong to interfere with such a process. Suppose a kitten is accidentally injected with the chemical. As long as it has not yet developed those properties that in themselves endow something with a right to life, there cannot be anything wrong with interfering with the causal process and preventing the development of the properties in question. Such interference might be accomplished either by injecting the kitten with some "neutralizing" chemical or simply by killing it.

But if it is not seriously wrong to destroy an injected kitten which will naturally develop the properties that bestow a right to life, neither can it be seriously wrong to destroy a member of Homo sapiens which lacks such properties, but will naturally come to have them. The potentialities are the same in both cases. The only difference is that in the case of a human fetus the potentialities have been present from the beginning of the organism's development, while in the case of the kitten they have been present only from the time it was injected with the special chemical. This difference in the time at which the potentialities were acquired is a morally irrelevant difference.

It should be emphasized that I am not here assuming that a human fetus does not possess properties which in themselves, and irrespective of their causal relationships to other properties, provide grounds for ascribing a right to life to whatever possesses them. The point is merely that if it is seriously wrong to kill something, the reason cannot be that the thing will later acquire properties that in themselves provide something with a right to life.

Finally, it is reasonable to believe that there are properties possessed by adult members of Homo sapiens which establish their right to life, and also that any normal human fetus will come to possess those properties shared by adult humans. But it has just been shown that if it is wrong to kill a human fetus, it cannot be because of its potentialities. One is therefore forced to conclude that the conservative's potentiality principle is false.

In short, anyone who wants to defend the potentiality principle must either argue against the moral symmetry principle or hold that in a world in which kittens could be transformed into "rational animals" it would be seriously wrong to kill newborn kittens. It is hard to believe there is much to be said for the latter moral claim. Consequently one expects the conservative's rejoinder to be directed against the symmetry principle. While I have not attempted to provide a thorough defense of that principle, I have tried to show that what seems to be the most important objection to it—the one that appeals to a distinction between positive and negative duties—is based on a superficial analysis of our moral intuitions. I believe that a more thorough examination of the symmetry principle would show it to be sound. If so, we should reject the potentiality principle, and the conservative position on abortion as well.

VI. SUMMARY AND CONCLUSIONS

Let us return now to my basic claim, the self-consciousness requirement: An organism possesses a serious right to life only if it possesses the concept of a self as a continuing subject of experiences and other mental states, and believes that it is itself such a continuing entity. My defense of this claim has been twofold. I have offered a direct argument in support of it, and I have tried to show that traditional conservative and liberal views on abortion and infanticide, which involve a rejection of it, are unsound. I now want to mention one final reason why my claim should be accepted. Consider the example mentioned in section II—that of killing, as opposed to torturing, newborn kittens. I suggested there that while in the case of adult humans most people would consider it worse to kill an individual than to torture him for an hour, we do not usually view the killing of a newborn kitten as morally outrageous, although we would regard someone who tortured a newborn kitten for an hour as heinously evil. I pointed out that a possible conclusion that might be drawn from this is that newborn kittens have a right not to be tortured, but do not have a serious right to life. If this is the correct conclusion, how is one to explain it? One merit of the self-consciousness requirement is that it provides an explanation of this situation. The reason a newborn kitten does not have a right to life is explained by the fact that it does not possess the concept of a self. But how is one to explain the kitten's having a right not to be tortured? The answer is that a desire not to suffer pain can be ascribed to something without assuming that it has any concept of a continuing self. For while something that lacks the concept of a self cannot desire that a self not suffer, it can desire that a given sensation not exist. The state desired—the absence of a particular sensation, or of sensations of a certain sort—can be described in a purely phenomenalistic language, and hence without the concept of a continuing self. So long as the newborn kitten possesses the relevant phenomenal concepts, it can truly be said to desire that a certain sensation not exist. So we can ascribe to it a right not to be tortured even though, since it lacks the concept of a continuing self, we cannot ascribe to it a right to life.

This completes my discussion of the basic moral principles involved in the issue of abortion and infanticide. But I want to comment upon an important factual question, namely, at what point an organism comes to possess the concept of a self as a continuing subject of experiences and other mental states, together with the belief that it is itself such a continuing entity. This is obviously a matter for detailed psychological investigation, but everyday observation makes it perfectly clear, I believe, that a newborn baby does not possess the concept of a continuing self, any more than a newborn kitten possesses such a concept. If so, infanticide during a time interval shortly after birth must be morally acceptable.

But where is the line to be drawn? What is the cutoff point? If one maintained, as some philosophers have, that an individual possesses concepts only if he can express these concepts in language, it would be a matter of everyday observation whether or not a given organism possessed the concept of a continuing self. Infanticide would then be permissible up to the time an organism learned how to use certain expressions. However, I think the claim that acquisition of concepts is dependent on acquisition of language is mistaken. For example, one wants to ascribe mental states of a conceptual sort—such as beliefs and desires—to organisms that are incapable of learning a language. This issue of prelinguistic understanding is clearly outside the scope of this discussion. My point is simply that *if* an organism can acquire concepts without thereby acquiring a way of expressing those concepts linguistically, the question of whether a given organism possesses the concept of a self as a continuing subject of experiences and other mental states, together with the belief that it is itself such a continuing entity, may be a question that requires fairly subtle experimental techniques to answer.

If this view of the matter is roughly correct, there are two worries one is left with at the level of practical moral decisions, one of which may turn out to be deeply disturbing. The lesser worry is where the line is to be drawn in the case of infanticide. It is not troubling because there is no serious need to know the exact point at which a human infant acquires a right to life. For in the vast majority of cases in which infanticide is desirable, its desirability will be apparent within a short time after birth. Since it is virtually certain that an infant at such a stage of its development does not possess the concept of a continuing self, and thus does not possess a serious right to life, there is excellent reason to believe that infanticide is morally permissible in most cases where it is otherwise desirable. The practical moral problem can thus be satisfactorily handled by choosing some period of time, such as a week after birth, as the interval during which infanticide will be permitted. This interval could then be modified once psychologists have established the point at which a human organism comes to believe that it is a continuing subject of experiences and other mental states.

The troubling worry is whether adult animals belonging to species other than Homo sapiens may not also possess a serious right to life. For once one says that an organism can possess the concept of a continuing self, together with the belief that it is itself such an entity, without having any way of expressing that concept and that belief linguistically, one has to face up to the question of whether animals may not possess properties that bestow a serious right to life upon them. The suggestion itself is a familiar one, and one that most of us are accustomed to dismiss very casually. The line of thought advanced here suggests that this attitude may turn out to be tragically mistaken. Once one reflects upon the question of the *basic* moral principles involved in the ascription of a right to life to organisms, one may find himself driven to conclude that our everyday treatment of animals is morally indefensible, and that we are in fact murdering innocent persons.

A Postscript   June 1973

The key to the question of the moral permissibility of abortion is, I think, the insight that there is a conceptual connection between the possession of a particular right and the capacity to have the corresponding desire. The claim that there is such a conceptual connection was supported by an analysis of the concept of a right and an account of the conditions under which an individual's right to something can be violated. The simplest suggestion as to the nature of this conceptual connection is that an action cannot violate an individual's right to something unless he has, at the time the action is performed, a desire for that thing. This account is, however, exposed to obvious counterexamples, and as a result I suggested that "an individual's right to X can be violated not only when he desires X, but also when he *would* now desire X were it not for one of the following: (i) he is in an emotionally unbalanced state; (ii) he is temporarily unconscious; (iii) he has been conditioned to desire the absence of X" (p. 63).

I believe that the basic contentions and the supporting arguments advanced in my defense of abortion and infanticide are essentially correct. However, it may be helpful to indicate very briefly the more important changes and additions I would make if I were revising the essay. A more detailed discussion of these points can be found in my response to criticisms in the Summer 1973 issue of *Philosophy & Public Affairs*.

The clauses dealing with emotionally unbalanced individuals and with individuals who have been subjected to conditioning which has "distorted" their desires are perhaps fair enough, for these are clearly exceptional cases, and it is not obvious exactly what account they should receive. But in the case of the temporarily unconscious individual one feels that it is an *ad hoc* modification simply to add a clause which says that an action can violate such an individual's right to something, even though he does not at the time have any desire for the thing. It would seem that a satisfactory account of rights should make clear the underlying rationale. If one fails to do this, a critic may well ask why one should make an exception of temporarily unconscious adults, but not of infants and fetuses.

I think that this problem can be dealt with by setting out a slightly more subtle account of the conditions under which an individual's rights can be violated. Such an account differs from that offered above by incorporating explicit reference to past and future desires. Leaving aside cases in which an individual's desires have been affected by lack of relevant information, or by emotional imbalance, or by his being subjected to abnormal physiological or psychological factors, one could then say that an individual's rights can be violated either by violating a corresponding desire which he now has, or, in appropriate circumstances, by violating a corresponding desire which he had at some time in the past, or will have at some time in the future.

The need to take into account past and future desires is shown by the fact that some present actions may violate, on the one hand, the rights of a dead person, and, on the other, the rights of future generations. For not only do these individuals fail to have the corresponding desire at the time the action is performed; they do not even exist.

Given this more complex but, I think, very natural account of the conceptual connection between rights and desires, the case of the temporarily unconscious individual becomes clear. If one kills such an individual one violates his right to life because one violates a desire he had before becoming unconscious: the desire to continue to exist as a subject of experiences and other mental states. The temporarily unconscious adult thus contrasts sharply with a human fetus or newborn infant, since the latter has not had, at any time past or present, a desire to continue to exist as a subject of experiences and other mental states. Consequently abortion and infanticide do not involve the violation of anyone's right to life.

The above revision also necessitates a slight change in the self-consciousness requirement which something must satisfy in order to have a right to life. In revised form, the self-consciousness requirement will state that an organism cannot have a serious right to life unless it either now possesses, or did possess at some time in the past, the concept of a self as a continuing subject of experiences and other mental states together with the belief that it is itself such an entity.

The other main revisions involve my discussion of the conservative position on abortion. First, there is a slight inaccuracy in my argument against the conservative position. I contended that the conservative position on abortion is defensible only if the potentiality principle is correct. The potentiality principle states that if there are properties possessed by normal adult human beings that endow any organism possessing them with a serious right to life, then at least one of those properties is such that any organism potentially possessing it has a serious right to life, simply by virtue of that potentiality. This conflicts with the account of rights offered earlier. A fertilized human egg cell has never had a desire to continue to exist as a subject of experiences and other mental states, nor is it the case that it would have had such a desire had it not been deprived of relevant information or subjected to abnormal influences. Therefore on the account of rights, it has no right to life, but on the potentiality principle, it appears to have such a right.

This problem can be avoided by revising the potentiality principle slightly. The principle should say, not that an organism that potentially possesses the relevant property has a right to life, but merely that in virtue of its potentiality, to kill such an organism is seriously wrong. (It is true that many people might be unwilling to accept this modification, since it implies that some actions are seriously wrong even though they do not violate anyone's right. This makes the question of *why* it is seriously wrong to kill a fetus a pressing one.)

This change does not substantially affect my objection to the conservative position. For the argument that I offer against the original version of the potentiality principle, based upon the moral symmetry principle, can easily be modified so that it is also an argument against the revised version.

It should be mentioned, however, that the original statement of my argument against the potentiality principle was somewhat imprecise at one point. Let me briefly restate the initial stages of the argument. Suppose that one has a special chemical that will, when injected into a kitten, slowly change its brain into one that is comparable to a human brain, and hence transform the kitten into an animal with all the psychological capabilities characteristic of normal adult human beings. It then follows from the moral symmetry principle that if one has a kitten which has been injected with the special chemical, but which has not had the time to develop the relevant psychological properties, it is no more seriously wrong to inject the kitten with some "neutralizing" chemical that will interfere with the process and thus prevent the kitten from developing the properties in question, than it would be to intentionally refrain from injecting a kitten with the special chemical.

What deserves emphasis is that it is not being assumed here that neither action is seriously wrong. What follows from the moral symmetry principle is simply that one action is no more wrong than the other. My original formulation of the argument was unclear and potentially misleading on this point.

The argument now proceeds as follows. Compare a kitten that has been injected with the special chemical, and then had the chemical neutralized before it could take effect, with a kitten that has not been injected with the special chemical. It is clear that it is no more seriously wrong to kill the former than to kill the latter. For although their bodies have undergone different processes in the past, this difference is morally irrelevant, and there need be no other differences between them, with respect either to present properties or potentialities.

Next, consider two kittens, one of which has been injected with the chemical, but has not yet developed those properties that in themselves would give it a right to life, and the other of which has not been injected with the chemical. It follows from the previous two steps in the argument that the combined action of injecting the first kitten with a neutralizing substance and then killing it is no more seriously wrong than the combined action of intentionally refraining from injecting the second kitten with the chemical, and then killing it. From this point on the argument will proceed as originally set out.

Finally, let me propose a second objection to the potentiality principle both in its original and revised versions. I believe that if one accepts the potentiality principle, one ought also to accept a generalized version of it. The generalized potentiality principle states that it is not only wrong to destroy *organisms* which have the appropriate potentialities, it is also seriously wrong to prevent *systems of objects*, which would normally develop the morally relevant properties in question, from doing so. For the contention would be that whether the potentialities reside in a single organism or in a system of interrelated objects is morally irrelevant. What matters is only that one is dealing with something that will, if not interfered with, develop the morally significant properties in question. To accept either the original or the revised version of the potentiality principle, while rejecting the generalized version of it, would seem to be an indefensible position.

If, however, one accepts the generalized potentiality principle, one will be forced to conclude that some methods of contraception are seriously wrong. It is true that some people who defend an extreme conservative position on abortion will find this a cheering conclusion. But I think that there are many more people who are conservatives on abortion who would want to reject, as completely unacceptable, the view that artificial contraception is seriously wrong. If my second argument is correct, such a combination of positions cannot successfully be defended. One must either accept the claim that some methods of contraception are seriously wrong, or else abandon the conservative position on abortion.

JOHN FINNIS

The Rights and Wrongs of Abortion

Fortunately, none of the arguments for and against abortion *need* be expressed in terms of "rights." As we shall see, Judith Thomson virtually admits as much in her "A Defense of Abortion."[1] But since she has chosen to conduct her case by playing off a "right to life" against a "right to decide what happens in and to one's body," I shall begin by showing how this way of arguing about the rights and wrongs of abortion needlessly complicates and confuses the issue. It is convenient and appropriate to speak of "rights" for purposes and in contexts which I shall try to identify; it is most inconvenient and inappropriate when one is debating the moral permissibility of types of action —types such as "abortions performed without the desire to kill," which is the type of action Thomson wishes to defend as morally permissible under most circumstances. So in section I of this essay I shall show how her specification and moral characterization of this type of action are logically independent of her discussion of "rights." Then in section II I shall outline some principles of moral characterization and of moral permissibility, principles capable of explaining some of the moral condemnations which Thomson expresses but which remain all too vulnerable and obscure in her paper. In section III I shall show how the elaboration of those principles warrants those condemnations of abortion which Thomson thinks mistaken as well as many of those attributions of human rights which she so much takes for granted. In section IV I briefly state the reason (misstated by Thomson and also

1. Pp. 3-22. Otherwise unidentified page references in the text are to this article.

by Wertheimer)² why the foetus from conception has human rights, i.e. should be given the same consideration as other human beings.

I

Thomson's reflections on rights develop in three stages. (A) She indicates a knot of problems about what rights are rights to; she dwells particularly on the problem "what it comes to, to have a right to life" (p. 11). (B) She indicates, rather less clearly, a knot of problems about the source of rights; in particular she suggests that, over a wide range (left unspecified by her) of types of right, a person has a right only to what he has "title" to by reason of some gift, concession, grant or undertaking to him by another person. (C) She cuts both these knots by admitting (but all too quietly) that her whole argument about abortion concerns simply what is "morally required" or "morally permissible"; that what is in question is really the scope and source of the mother's responsibility (and only derivatively, by entailment, the scope and source of the unborn child's rights). I shall now examine these three stages a little more closely, and then (D) indicate why I think it useful to have done so.

(A) How do we specify the content of a right? What is a right a right to? Thomson mentions at least nine different rights which a person might rightly or wrongly be said to have.³ Of these nine, seven

2. Pp. 23-51.
3. Rights which Thomson is willing to allow that a person has:

R1. a right to life (p. 7);
R2. a right to decide what happens in and to one's body (p. 6) (to be equated, apparently, with a just prior claim to one's own body, p. 10);
R3. a right to defend oneself (i.e. to self-defense, p. 9);
R4. a right to refuse to lay hands on other people (even when it would be just and fair to do so, p. 10)—more precisely, a right not to lay hands on other people. . . .

Rights which she thinks it would be coherent but mistaken to claim that a person has or in any event always has:

R5. a right to demand that someone else give one assistance (p. 19)—more precisely, a right to be given assistance by . . . ;
R6. a right to be given whatever one needs for continued life (p. 11);
R7. a right to the use of (or to be given, or to be allowed to continue, the use of) someone else's body (or house) (p. 12);

have the same logical structure;[4] viz., in each instance, the alleged
right is a right with respect to P's action (performance, omission) as
an action which may affect Q. In some of these seven instances,[5] the
right with respect to P's action is P's right (which Hohfeld[6] called a
privilege and Hohfeldians call a liberty). In the other instances,[7] the
right with respect to P's action is Q's right (which Hohfeldians call a
"claim-right"). But in all these seven instances there is what I shall
call a "Hohfeldian right": to assert a Hohfeldian right is to assert a
three-term relation between two persons and the action of one of those
persons insofar as that action concerns the other person.

The other two rights mentioned by Thomson have a different logical
structure.[8] In both these instances, the alleged right is a right with
respect to a thing (one's "own body," or the state of affairs referred
to as one's "life"). Here the relation is two-term: between one person
and some thing or state of affairs. Rights in this sense cannot be completely analyzed in terms of some unique combination of Hohfeldian
rights.[9] P's right to a thing (land, body, life) can and normally should
be secured by granting or attributing Hohfeldian rights to him or to
others; but just which combination of such Hohfeldian rights will
properly or best secure his single right to the thing in question will
vary according to time, place, person and circumstance. And since
moral judgments centrally concern *actions*, it is this specification of
Hohfeldian rights that we need for moral purposes, rather than in-
vocations of rights to things.

Since Thomson concentrates on the problematic character of the
"right to life," I shall illustrate what I have just said by reference to
the "right to one's own body," which she should (but seems, in prac-

---

R8. a right not to be killed by anybody (p. 12);

R9. a right to slit another's throat (an instance, apparently, of a "right to
be guaranteed his death") (p. 22).

4. Namely, R3 through R9 in the list of note 3 above.

5. Namely, R3, R4 and, in one of their senses, R7 and R9.

6. W. N. Hohfeld, *Fundamental Legal Conceptions* (New Haven, 1923).

7. Namely, R5, R6, R8 and, in another of their senses, R7 and R9.

8. Namely, R1 and R2.

9. This proposition is elaborated in a juridical context by A. M. Honoré,
"Rights of Exclusion and Immunities against Divesting," *University of Tulane
Law Review* 34 (1960): 453.

tice, not to) regard as equally problematic. Now her two explicit versions of this right are: one's "just, prior claim to his own body," and one's "right to decide what happens in and to one's body." But both versions need much specification[10] before they can warrant moral judgments about particular sorts of action. For example, the "right to decide" may be *either* (i) a right (Hohfeldian liberty) to do things to or with one's own body (e.g. to remove those kidney plugs, or that baby, from it—but what else? anything? do I have the moral liberty to decide not to raise my hand to the telephone to save Kitty Genovese from her murderers? cf. pp. 18-19); *or* (ii) a right (Hohfeldian claim-right) that other people shall not (at least without one's permission) do things to or with one's own body (e.g. draw sustenance from, or inhabit, it—but what else? anything?); *or* (iii) some combination of these forms of right with each other or with other forms of right such as (a) the right (Hohfeldian power) to change another person's right (liberty) to use one's body by making a grant of or permitting such use (*any* such use?), or (b) the right (Hohfeldian immunity) not to have one's right (claim-right) to be free from others' use of one's body diminished or affected by purported grants or permissions by third parties. And as soon as we thus identify these possible sorts of right, available to give concrete moral content to the "right to one's body," it becomes obvious that the actions which the right entitles, disentitles or requires one to perform (or entitles, disentitles or requires others to perform) *vary* according to the identity and circumstances of the two parties to each available and relevant Hohfeldian

10. Insufficient specification causes needless problems, besides those mentioned in the text. For example, against "so using the term 'right' that from the fact that A ought to do a thing for B, it follows that B has a right against A that A do it for him," Thomson objects that any such use of the term "right" is "going to make the question of whether or not a man has a right to a thing turn on how easy it is to provide him with it" (pp. 16-17); and she adds that it's "rather a shocking idea that anybody's rights should fade away and disappear as it gets harder and harder to accord them to him" (p. 17). So she says she has no "right" to the touch of Henry Fonda's cool hand, *because*, although he ought to cross the room to touch her brow (and thus save her life), he is not morally obliged to cross America to do so. But this objection rests merely on inadequate specification of the right as against Henry Fonda. For if we say that she has a right that Henry Fonda should cross-the-room-to-touch-her-fevered-brow, and that she has no right that he should cross-America-to-touch-her-fevered-brow, then we can (if we like!) continue to deduce rights from duties.

right. And this, though she didn't recognize it, is the reason why Thomson found the "right to life" problematic, too.

(B) I suspect it was her concentration on non-Hohfeldian rights ("title" to things like chocolates or bodies) that led Thomson to make the curious suggestion which appears and reappears, though with a very uncertain role, in her paper. I mean, her suggestion that we should speak of "rights" only in respect of what a man has "title" to (usually, if not necessarily, by reason of gift, concession or grant to him).

This suggestion,[11] quite apart from the dubious centrality it accords to ownership and property in the spectrum of rights, causes needless confusion in the presentation of Thomson's defense of abortion. For if the term "right" were to be kept on the "tight rein" which she suggests (p. 16), then (a) the Popes and others whose appeal to "the right to life" she is questioning would deprive her paper of its starting point and indeed its pivot by simply rephrasing their appeal so as to eliminate all reference to rights (for, as I show in the next section, they are not alleging that the impropriety of abortion follows from any grant, gift or concession of "rights" to the unborn child); and (b) Thomson would likewise have to rephrase claims she herself makes, such as that innocent persons certainly have a right to life, that moth-

11. It is perhaps worth pointing out that, even if we restrict our attention to the rights involved in gifts, concessions, grants, contracts, trusts and the like, Thomson's proposed reining-in of the term "right" will be rather inconvenient. Does only the donee have the "rights"? Suppose that uncle U gives a box of chocolates to nephew N1, with instructions to share it with nephew N2, and asks father F to see that this sharing is done. Then we want to be able to say that U has a right that N1 and N2 shall each get their share, that N1 shall give N2 that share, that F shall see to it that this is done, and so on; and that N1 has the right to his share, the right not to be interfered with by F or N2 or anyone else in eating his share, and so on; and that N2 has a similar set of rights; and that F has the right to take steps to enforce a fair distribution, the right not to be interfered with in taking those steps, and so on. Since disputes may arise about any one of these relations between the various persons and their actions and the chocolates thereby affected, it is convenient to have the term "right" on a loose rein, to let it ride round the circle of relations, picking up the action in dispute and fitting the competing claims about "the right thing to do" into intelligible and typical three-term relationships. Yet some of the rights involved in the gift of the chocolates, for example U's rights, are not acquired by any grant to the right-holder.

ers have the right to abort themselves to save their lives, that P has a right not to be tortured to death by Q even if R is threatening to kill Q unless Q does so, and so on. But if such rephrasing is possible (as indeed it is), then it is obvious that suggestions about the proper or best way to use the term "a right" are irrelevant to the substantive moral defense or critique of abortion.

But this terminological suggestion is linked closely with Thomson's substantive thesis that we do not have any "special [scil. Good Samaritan or Splendid Samaritan] responsibility" for the life or well-being of others "unless we have assumed it, explicitly or implicitly" (p. 21). It is this (or some such) thesis about *responsibility* on which Thomson's whole argument, in the end, rests.

(C) Thomson's explicit recognition that her defense of abortion *need* not have turned on the assertion or denial of rights comes rather late in her paper, when she says that there is "no need to insist on" her suggested reined-in use of the term "right":   •

> If anyone does wish to deduce "he has a right" from "you ought," then all the same he must surely grant that there are cases in which it is not morally required of you that you allow that violinist to use your kidneys. . . .[12] And so also for mother and unborn child. Except in such cases as the unborn person has a right to demand it . . . nobody is morally *required* to make large sacrifices . . . in order to keep another person alive (pp. 17-18).

In short, the dispute is about what is "morally required" (i.e. about what one "must" and, for that matter, "may" or "can" [not] do: see p. 52); that is to say, about the rights and wrongs of abortion. True, on page 61 there is still that "right to demand large sacrifices" cluttering up the margins of the picture. But when we come to the last pages of her paper (pp. 20-21) even that has been set aside, and the real

12. The sentence continues: "and in which he does not have a right to use them, and in which you do not do him an injustice if you refuse." But these are merely remnants of the "rhetoric" in which she has cast her argument. Notice, incidentally, that her suggestion that "justice" and "injustice" should be restricted to respect for and violation of rights in her reined-in sense is of no importance since she grants that actions not in her sense unjust may be self-centered, callous and indecent, and that these vices are "no less grave" (p. 17).

question is identified as not whether the child has a "right to demand large sacrifices" of its mother, but whether the mother has a "special responsibility" to or for the child (since, if she has, then she may be morally required to make large sacrifices for it and *therefore* we will be able to assert, by a convenient locution, the child's "right to [demand] those sacrifices").

(D) So in the end most of the argument about rights was a red herring. I have bothered to track down this false trail, not merely to identify some very common sorts and sources of equivocation (more will come to light in the next two sections), but also to show how Thomson's decision to conduct her defense in terms of "rights" makes it peculiarly easy to miss a most important weak point in her defense. This weak point is the connection or relation between one's "special responsibilities" and one's ordinary (not special) responsibilities; and one is enabled to miss it easily if one thinks (a) that the whole problem is essentially one of rights, (b) that rights typically or even essentially depend on grant, concession, assumption, etc., (c) that special responsibilities likewise depend on grants, concessions, assumptions, etc., and (d) that therefore the whole moral problem here concerns one's *special* responsibilities. Such a train of thought is indeed an enthymeme, if not a downright fallacy; but that is not surprising, since I am commenting here not on an argument offered by Thomson but on a likely effect of her "rhetoric."

What Thomson, then, fails to attend to adequately is the claim (one of the claims implicit, I think, in the papal and conservative rhetoric of rights) that the mother's duty not to abort herself is *not* an incident of any special responsibility which she assumed or undertook for the child, but is a straightforward incident of an ordinary duty everyone owes to his neighbor. Thomson indeed acknowledges that such ordinary nonassumed duties exist and are as morally weighty as duties of justice in her reined-in sense of "justice"; but I cannot discern the principles on which she bases, and (confidently) delimits the range of, these duties.[13]

13. Perhaps this is the point at which to note how dubious is Thomson's assertion that "in no state in this country is any man compelled by law to be even a Minimally Decent Samaritan to any person," and her insinuation that this is a manifestation of discrimination against women. This sounds so odd

She speaks, for instance, about "the drastic limits to the right of self-defense": "If someone threatens you with death unless you torture someone else to death, I think you have not the right, even to save your life, to do so" (p. 9). Yet she also says: "If anything in the world is true, it is that you do not . . . do what is impermissible, if you reach around to your back and unplug yourself from that violinist to save your life" (p. 8). So why, in the first case, has one the strict responsibility not to bring about the death demanded? Surely she is not suggesting that the pain ("torture") makes the difference, or that it *is* morally permissible to kill *painlessly* another person on the orders of a third party who threatens you with death for noncompliance? And, since she thinks that "nobody is morally *required* to make large sacrifices, of health, of all other interests and concerns, of all other duties and commitments, for nine years, or even for nine months, in order to keep another person alive" (p. 18), will she go on to say that it is permissible, when a third party threatens you with such "large sacrifices" (though well short of your life), to *kill* (painlessly) another person, or two or ten other persons?

If Thomson balks at such suggestions, I think it must be because she does in the end rely on some version of the distinction, forced underground in her paper, between "direct killing" and "not keeping another person alive."

The more one reflects on Thomson's argument, the more it seems to turn and trade on some version of this distinction. Of course she starts by rejecting the view that it is always wrong to directly kill, because that view would (she thinks) condemn one to a lifetime plugged into the violinist. But she proceeds, as we have noted, to reject at least one form of killing to save one's life, on grounds that seem to have nothing to do with consequences and everything to do with the formal

coming from a country in which a young man, not a young woman, is compelled by law to "give up long stretches of his life" to defending his country at considerable "risk of death for himself." True, he is not doing this for "a person who has no special right to demand it"; indeed, what makes active military service tough is that one is not risking one's life to save *anybody* in particular from any *particular* risk. And are we to say that young men have *assumed* a "special responsibility" for defending other people? Wouldn't that be a gross fiction which only a lame moral theory could tempt us to indulge in? But it is just this sort of social contractarianism that Thomson is tempting us with.

context and thus structure of one's action (the sort of formal considerations that usually are wrapped up, as we shall see, in the word "direct"). And indeed the whole movement of her argument in defense of abortion is to assimilate abortion to the range of Samaritan problems, on the basis that having an abortion is, or can be, justified as *merely* a way of *not rendering special assistance*. Again, the argument turns, not on a calculus of consequences, but on the formal characteristics of one's choice itself.

Well, why should this apparently *formal* aspect of one's choice determine one's precise responsibilities in a certain situation whatever the other circumstances and expected consequences or upshots? When we know *why*, on both sides of the debate about abortion, we draw and rely on these distinctions, then we will be better placed to consider (i) whether or not unplugging from the violinist is, after all, direct killing in the sense alleged to be relevant by Popes and others, and (ii) whether or not abortion is, after all, just like unplugging the captive philosopher from the moribund musician.

II

Like Thomson's moral language (setting off the "permissible" against the "impermissible"), the traditional rule about killing doubtless gets its peremptory sharpness primarily (historically speaking) from the injunction, respected as divine and revealed: "Do not kill the innocent and just."[14] But the handful of peremptory negative moral principles correspond to the handful of really basic aspects of human flourishing, which in turn correspond to the handful of really basic and controlling human needs and human inclinations. To be fully reasonable, one must remain *open* to every basic aspect of human flourishing, to every basic form of human good. For is not each irreducibly basic, and none merely means to end? Are not the basic goods incommensurable? Of course it is reasonable to concentrate on realizing those forms of good, in or for those particular communities and persons (first of all oneself), which one's situation, talents and opportunities most fit one for. But concentration, specialization, particularization is one thing; it is quite another thing, rationally and thus

14. Exodus 23:7; cf. Exodus 20:13, Deuteronomy 5:17, Genesis 9:6, Jeremiah 7:6 and 22:3.

morally speaking, to make a choice which cannot but be characterized
as a choice *against* life (to kill), *against* communicable knowledge
of truth (to lie, where truth is at stake in communication), *against*
procreation, *against* friendship and the justice that is bound up with
friendship. Hence the strict negative precepts.[15]

The general sense of "responsibility," "duty," "obligation," "permissibility" is not my concern here, but rather the *content* of our responsibilities, duties, obligations, of the demands which human good makes
on each of us. The general demand is that we remain adequately open
to, attentive to, respectful of, and willing to pursue human good insofar as it can be realized and respected in our choices and dispositions.
Now most moral failings are not by way of violation of strict negative
precepts—i.e. are not straightforward choices against basic values.
Rather, they are forms of negligence, of *insufficient* regard for these
basic goods, or for the derivative structures reasonably created to support the basic goods. And when someone is accused of violating directly a basic good, he will usually plead that he was acting out of a
proper care and concern for the realization of that or another basic
value in the *consequences* of his chosen act though not in the act itself.
For example, an experimenter accused of killing children in order to
conduct medical tests will point out that these deaths are necessary to
these tests, and these tests to medical discoveries, and the discoveries
to the saving of many more lives—so that, in view of the foreseeable
consequences of his deed, he displays (he will argue) a fully adequate
(indeed, the only adequate) and reasonable regard for the value of
human life.

But to appeal to consequences in this fashion is to set aside one
criterion of practical reasonableness and hence of morality—namely,
that one remain open to each basic value, and attentive to some basic
value, in each of one's chosen acts—in favor of quite another criterion
—namely, that one choose so to act as to bring about consequences
involving a greater balance of good over bad than could be expected
to be brought about by doing any alternative action open to one. Hare

15. These remarks are filled out somewhat in my "Natural Law and Unnatural Acts," *Heythrop Journal* 11 (1970): 365. See also Germain Grisez,
Abortion: the Myths, the Realities and the Arguments (New York 1970), chap.
6. My argument owes much to this and other works by Grisez.

has observed that *"for practical purposes* there is no important difference" between most of the currently advocated theories in ethics;
they all are "utilitarian," a term he uses to embrace Brandt's ideal observer theory, Richards's (Rawls's?) rational contractor theory, specific rule-utilitarianism, universalistic act-utilitarianism and his own
universal prescriptivism.[16] All justify and require, he argues, the adoption of "the principles whose general inculcation will have, all in all,
the best consequences."[17] I offer no critique of this utilitarianism here;
Thomson's paper is not, on its face, consequentialist. Suffice it to in-
quire how Hare and his fellow consequentialists know the future that
to most of us is hidden. How do they know what unit of computation
to select from among the incommensurable and irreducible basic aspects of human flourishing; what principle of distribution of goods
to commend to an individual considering his own interests, those of
his friends, his family, his enemies, his *patria* and those of all men
present and future? How do they know how to define the "situation"
whose universal specification will appear in the principle whose adoption (singly? in conjunction with other principles?) "will" have best
consequences;[18] whether and how to weigh future and uncertain consequences against present and certain consequences? And how do
they know that net good consequences would in fact be maximized
(even if *per impossibile* they were calculable) by general adoption of
consequentialist principles of action along with consequentialist "principles" to justify nonobservance of consequentialist "principles" in
"hard cases"?[19] One cannot understand the Western moral tradition,
with its peremptory negative (forbearance-requiring) principles (the
positive principles being relevant in all, but peremptory in few, particular situations), unless one sees why that tradition rejected consequentialism as mere self-delusion—for Hare and his fellow consequentialists can provide no satisfactory answer to any of the foregoing
lines of inquiry, and have no coherent rational account to give of any

16. R. M. Hare, "Rules of War and Moral Reasoning," *Philosophy & Public
Affairs* 1, no. 2 (Winter 1972): 167, 168.

17. *Ibid.*, p. 174.

18. Cf. H.-N. Castañeda, "On the Problem of Formulating a Coherent Act-
Utilitarianism," *Analysis* 32 (1972): 118; Harold M. Zellner, "Utilitarianism
and Derived Obligation," *Analysis* 32 (1972): 124.

19. See D. H. Hodgson, *Consequences of Utilitarianism* (Oxford, 1967).

level of moral thought above that of the man who thinks how good it would be to act "for the best."[20] Expected total consequences of one's action do not provide a sufficient ground for making a choice that cannot but be regarded as *itself* a choice directly against a basic value (even that basic value which it is hoped will be realized in the *consequences*)—for expected total consequences cannot be given an evaluation sufficiently reasonable and definitive to be the decisive measure of our response to the call of human values, while a choice directly against a basic good provides, one might say, its own definitive evaluation of itself.

I do not expect these isolated and fragmentary remarks to be in themselves persuasive. I do not deny that the traditional Western willingness, (in theory) to discount expected consequences wherever the action itself could not but be characterized as against a basic value, is or was supported by the belief that Providence would inevitably provide that "all manner of things shall be well" (i.e. that the whole course of history would turn out to have been a fine thing, indisputably evil deeds and their consequences turning out to have been "all to the good" like indisputably saintly deeds and their consequences). Indeed, the consequentialist moralist, who nourishes his moral imagination on scenarios in which by killing an innocent or two he saves scores, thousands, millions or even the race itself, rather obviously is a post-Christian phenomenon—such an assumption of the role of Providence would have seemed absurd to the pre-Christian philosophers[21] known to Cicero and Augustine. I am content to suggest the theoretical and moral context in which the casuistry of "direct" and "indirect" develops, within the wider context of *types* of action to be considered "impermissible" (I leave the term incompletely accounted for) because *inescapably* (i.e. whatever the hoped-for consequences) choices *against*

20: Cf. Hare, "Rules of War and Moral Reasoning," p. 174: "The defect in most deontological theories . . . is that they have no coherent rational account to give of any level of moral thought above that of the man who knows some good simple moral principles and sticks to them. . . . [The] simple principles of the deontologist . . . are what we should be trying to inculcate into ourselves and our children if we want to stand the best chance . . . of doing what is for the best."

21. Not to mention the Jewish moralists: see D. Daube, *Collaboration with Tyranny in Rabbinic Law* (Oxford, 1965).

a basic value of human living and doing. In short, one's responsibility
for the realization of human good, one's fostering of or respect for
human flourishing in future states of affairs at some greater or lesser
remove from one's present action, does not override one's responsibility to respect each basic form of human good which comes directly
in question in one's present action itself.

But how does one choose "directly against" a basic form of good?
When is it the case, for example, that one's choice, one's intentional
act, "cannot but be" characterized as "inescapably" anti-life? Is abortion always (or ever) such a case? A way to tackle these questions can
be illustrated by reference to three hard cases whose traditional "solutions" contributed decisively to the traditional judgment about abortion. The relevance of these "hard cases" and "solutions" to the
discussion with Thomson should be apparent in each case, but will
become even more apparent in the next section.

(i) *Suicide.* Considered as a fully deliberate choice (which it
doubtless only rather rarely is), suicide is a paradigm case of an action
that is always wrong because it cannot but be characterized as a choice ✓
directly against a fundamental value, life. The characterization is
significant, for what makes the killing of oneself attractive is usually,
no doubt, the prospect of peace, relief, even a kind of freedom or personal integration, and sometimes is an admirable concern for others;
but no amount of concentration on the allure of these positive values
can disguise from a clear-headed practical reasoner that it is *by* and *in*
killing himself that he intends or hopes to realize those goods. And the
characterization is given sharpness and definition by the contrast with
heroic self-sacrifices in battle or with willing martyrdom.[22] Where
Durkheim treated martyrdom as a case of suicide,[23] anybody concerned with the intentional structure of actions (rather than with a
simplistic analysis of movements with foreseen upshots) will grant
that the martyr is not directly choosing death, either as end or as

22. Note that I am not asserting (or denying) that self-sacrificial heroism
and martyrdom are moral duties; I am explaining why they need not be regarded
as moral faults.
23. *Le Suicide* (Paris, 1897), p. 5. Cf. also Daube's remarks on Donne in
"The Linguistics of Suicide," *Philosophy & Public Affairs* 1, no. 4 (Summer
1972): pp. 418ff.

means. For, however certainly death may be expected to ensue from the martyr's choice not to accede to the tyrant's threats, still it will ensue through, and as the point of, *someone else's* deliberate act (the tyrant's or the executioner's), and thus the martyr's chosen act of defiance need not be interpreted as itself a choice against the good of life.

The case of suicide has a further significance. The judgments, the characterizations and the distinctions made in respect of someone's choices involving his *own* death will be used in respect of choices involving the death of *others*. In other words, *rights* (such as the "right to life") are not the fundamental rationale for the judgment that the killing of other (innocent) persons is impermissible. What is impermissible is an intention set against the value of human life where that value is directly at stake in any action by virtue of the intentional and causal structure of that action; and such an impermissible intention may concern my life or yours—and no one speaks of his "right to life" as against himself, as something that would explain why *his* act of self-killing would be wrongful.

Indeed, I think the real justification for speaking of "rights" is to make the point that, when it comes to characterizing intentional actions in terms of their openness to basic human values, those human values are, and are to be, realized in the lives and well-being of others as well as in the life and well-being of the actor. That is, the point of speaking of "rights" is to stake out the relevant claims to equality and nondiscrimination (claims that are not to absolute equality, since *my* life and my well-being have some reasonable priority in the direction of *my* practical effort, if only because I am better placed to secure them). But the claims are to equality of *treatment*; so, rather than speak emptily of (say) a "right to life," it would be better to speak of (say, inter alia) a "right not to be killed intentionally"—where the meaning and significance of "intentional killing" can be illuminated by consideration of the right and wrong of killing oneself (i.e. of a situation where no "rights" are in question and one is alone with the bare problem of the right relation between one's acts and the basic values that can be realized or spurned in human actions).

Finally, the case of suicide and its traditional solution remind us forcefully that traditional Western ethics simply does not accept that

a person has "a right to decide what shall happen in and to his body,"
a right which Thomson thinks, astonishingly (since she is talking of
Pius XI and Pius XII), that "everybody seems to be ready to grant"
(p. 6). Indeed, one might go so far as to say that traditional Western
ethics holds that, because and to the extent that one does *not* have
the "right" to decide what shall happen in and to one's body, one
therefore and to that extent does not have the right to decide what
shall, by way of one's own acts, happen in and to anyone else's body.
As I have already hinted, and shall elaborate later, this would be something of an oversimplification, since one's responsibility for one's own
life, health etc. is reasonably regarded as prior to one's concern for
the life, health etc. of others. But the oversimplification is worth risking in order to make the point that the traditional condemnation of
abortion (as something one makes happen in and to a baby's body)
starts by rejecting what Thomson thinks everyone will admit.

(ii) *D's killing an innocent V in order to escape death at the hands
of P, who has ordered D to kill V.* This case has been traditionally
treated on the same footing as cases such as D's killing V in order to
save Q (or $Q_1, Q_2 \ldots Q_n$) from death (perhaps at the hands of P) or
from disease (where D is a medical researcher); for all such cases
cannot but be characterized as choices to act directly against human
life. Of course, in each case, the reason for making the choice is to
save life; but such saving of life will be effected, if at all, through the
choices of other actors (e.g. P's choice not to kill D where D has killed
V; or P's choice not to kill Q) or through quite distinct sequences of
events (e.g. Q's being given life-saving drugs discovered by D).

Hence the traditional ethics affirms that "there are drastic limits to
the right of self-defense" in much the same terms as Thomson. "If
someone threatens you with death when you torture someone else to
death . . . you have not the right, even to save your own life, to do so"
(p. 9). And it was this very problem that occasioned the first ecclesiastical pronouncement on abortion in the modern era, denying that
"it is licit to procure abortion before animation of the foetus in order
to prevent a girl, caught pregnant, being killed or dishonored."[24] The

24. Decree of the Holy Office, 2 March 1679, error no. 34; see Denzinger and
Schönmetzer, *Enchiridion symbolorum definitionum et declarationum de rebus*

choice to abort here cannot but be characterized as a choice against life, since its intended good life- or reputation-saving effects are merely expected consequences, occurring if at all through the further acts of other persons, and thus are not what is being *done* in and by the act of abortion itself. But I do not know how one could arrive at any view of this second sort of hard case by juggling, as Thomson seems to be willing to, with a "right to life," a "right to determine what happens in and to your own body," a "right of self-defense" and a "right to refuse to lay hands on other people"—all rights shared equally by D, V, P, and Q, Q_1, Q_2 . . . !

(iii) *Killing the mother to save the child.* This was the only aspect of abortion that Thomas Aquinas touched on, but he discussed it thrice.[25] For if it is accepted that eternal death is worse than mere bodily death, shouldn't one choose the lesser evil? So if the unborn child is likely to die unbaptized, shouldn't one open up the mother, rip out the child and save-it-from-eternal-death-by-baptizing-it? (If you find Aquinas's problem unreal, amend it—consider instead the cases where the child's life seems so much more valuable, whether to itself or to others, than the life of its sick or old or low-born mother.) No, says Aquinas. He evidently considers (for reasons I consider in section III) that the project involves a direct choice against life and is straightforwardly wrong, notwithstanding the good consequences.

So the traditional condemnation of therapeutic abortion flows not from a prejudice against women or in favor of children but from a straightforward application of the solution in the one case to the other case, on the basis that mother and child are *equally* persons in whom the value of human life is to be realized (or the "right to life" respected) and not directly attacked.[26]

---

fidei et morum (Barcelona, 1967), par. 2134; Grisez, *Abortion: the Myths, the Realities and the Arguments*, p. 174; John T. Noonan, Jr., "An Almost Absolute Value in History," in *The Morality of Abortion*, ed. John T. Noonan, Jr. (Cambridge, Mass., 1970), p. 34.

25. See *Summa Theologiae* III, q.68, art. 11; *in 4 Sententiarum* d.6, q.1. a.1, q.1, ad 4; d.23, q.2, a.2, q.1, ad 1 & 2; Grisez, *op. cit.*, p. 154; Noonan, *op. cit.*, p. 24.

26. Pius XII's remark, quoted by Thomson, that "the baby in the maternal breast has the right to life immediately from God" has its principal point, not

III

But now at last let us look at this "traditional condemnation of abortion" a little more closely than Thomson does. It is not a condemnation of the administration of medications to a pregnant mother whose life is threatened by, say, a high fever (whether brought on by pregnancy or not), in an effort to reduce the fever, even if it is known that such medications have the side effect of inducing miscarriage. It is not a condemnation of the removal of the malignantly cancerous womb of a pregnant women, even if it is known that the foetus within is not of viable age and so will die. It is quite doubtful whether it is a condemnation of an operation to put back in its place the displaced womb of a pregnant woman whose life is threatened by the displacement, even though the operation necessitates the draining off of the amniotic fluids necessary to the survival of the foetus.[27]

But why are these operations not condemned? As Foot has remarked, the distinction drawn between these and other death-dealing operations "has evoked particularly bitter reactions on the part of non-Catholics. If you are permitted to bring about the death of the child, what does it matter how it is done?"[28] Still, she goes some way to answering her own question; she is not content to let the matter rest where Hart had left it, when he said:

> Perhaps the most perplexing feature of these cases is that the overriding aim in all of them is the same good result, namely . . . to save the mother's life. The differences between the cases are differences of causal structure leading to the applicability of different verbal distinctions. There seems to be no relevant moral difference between them on any theory of morality . . . [to attribute

---

(*pace* Thomson, p. 7) in the assertion of a premise from which one could deduce the wrongfulness of direct killing, but in the assertion that *if* anybody—e.g. the mother—has the right not to be directly killed, *then* the baby has the same right, since as Pius XII goes on immediately "the baby, still not born, is a man in the same degree and for the same reason as the mother."

27. The three cases mentioned in this paragraph are discussed in a standard and conservative Roman Catholic textbook: Marcellino Zalba, *Theologiae Moralis Compendium* (Madrid, 1958), I, p. 885.

28. Philippa Foot, "The Problem of Abortion and the Doctrine of Double Effect," *The Oxford Review* 5 (1967): 6.

moral relevance to distinctions drawn in this way] in cases where the ultimate purpose is the same can only be explained as the result of a legalistic conception of morality as if it were conceived in the form of a law in rigid form prohibiting all intentional killing as distinct from knowingly causing death.[29]

Foot recognizes that attention to "overriding aim" and "ultimate purpose" is not enough if we are to keep clear of moral horrors such as saving life by killing innocent hostages, etc. As a general though not exclusive and not (it seems) at-all-costs principle, she proposes that one has a duty to refrain from doing injury to innocent people and that this duty is stricter than one's duty to aid others; this enables her to see that "we might find" the traditional conclusion correct, that we must not crush the unborn child's skull in order to save the mother (in a case where the child could be saved if one let the mother die): "for in general we do not think that we can kill one innocent person to rescue another."[30] But what is it to "do injury to" innocent people? She does not think it an injury to blow a man to pieces, or kill and eat him, in order to save others trapped with him in a cave, *if he is certain to die soon anyway.*[31] So I suppose that, after all, she *would* be willing (however reluctantly) to justify the killing by D of hostages, V, V_1, V_2, whenever the blackmailer P threatened to kill *them too*, along with Q, Q_1, Q_2, unless D killed them himself. One wonders whether this is not an unwarranted though plausible concession to consequentialism.

In any event, Foot was aware, not only that the "doctrine of the double effect" "should be taken seriously in spite of the fact that it sounds rather odd . . . ,"[32] but also of what Thomson has not recorded in her brief footnote (p. 6 n. 3) on the technical meaning given to the term "direct" by moralists using the "doctrine" to analyze the relation between choices and basic values, namely that the "doctrine" requires more than that a certain bad effect or aspect (say, someone's being killed) of one's deed be not intended either as end or as means. If one is to establish that one's death-dealing deed need not be char-

29. H.L.A. Hart, "Intention and Punishment," *The Oxford Review* 4 (1967): 13; reprinted in Hart, *Punishment and Responsibility* (Oxford, 1968), pp. 124-125.

30. Foot, "The Problem of Abortion and the Doctrine of Double Effect," p. 15
31. *Ibid.*, p. 14.   32. *Ibid.*, p. 8.

acterized as directly or intentionally against the good of human life, ✓
the "doctrine" requires further that the good effect or aspect, which *is*
intended, should be proportionate (say, saving someone's life), i.e.
sufficiently good and important relative to the bad effect or aspect:
otherwise (we may add, in our own words) one's choice, although not
directly and intentionally to kill, will reasonably be counted as a
choice inadequately open to the value of life.[33] And this consideration
alone might well suffice to rule out abortions performed in order simply to remove the unwanted foetus from the body of women who conceived as a result of forcible rape, even if one were to explicate the
phrase "intended directly as end or as means" in such a way that the
abortion did not amount to a directly intended killing (e.g. because
the mother desired only the removal, not the death of the foetus, and
would have been willing to have the foetus reared in an artificial womb
had one been available).[34]

Well, how *should* one explicate these central requirements of the
"doctrine" of double effect? When *should* one say that the expected
bad effect or aspect of an action is not intended either as end or as
means and hence does not determine the moral character of the act
as a choice not to respect one of the basic human values? Since it
is in any case impossible to undertake a full discussion of this question here, let me narrow the issue down to the more difficult and con-
troverted problem of "means." Clearly enough, D intends the death of
V *as a means* when he kills him in order to conform to the orders of
the blackmailer P (with the object of thereby saving the lives of Q
et al.), since the good effect of D's act will follow only by virtue of
another human act (here P's). But Grisez (no consequentialist!)
argues that the bad effects or aspects of some *natural* process or chain

33. *Ibid.*, p. 7. This is the fourth of the four usual conditions for the application of the "Doctrine of Double Effect"; see e.g. Grisez, *Abortion: the Myths,
the Realities and the Arguments*, p. 329. G.E.M. Anscombe, "War and Murder,"
in *Nuclear Weapons and Christian Conscience*, ed. W. Stein, (London, 1961),
p. 57, formulates the "principle of double effect," in relation to the situation
where "someone innocent will die unless I do a wicked thing," thus: "you are
no murderer if a man's death was neither your aim nor your chosen means,
*and if you had to act in the way that led to it or else do something absolutely
forbidden*" (emphasis added).

34. Grisez argues thus, *op. cit.*, p. 343; also in "Toward a Consistent Natural-
Law Ethics of Killing," *American Journal of Jurisprudence* 15 (1970): 95.

of causation need not be regarded as intended as means to the good effects or aspects of that process even if the good effects or aspects *depend* on them in the causal sense (and provided that those good effects could not have been attained in some other way by that agent in those circumstances).[35] So he would, I think, say that Thomson could rightly unplug herself from the violinist (at least where the hook-up endangered her life) even if "unplugging" could only be effected by chopping the violinist in pieces. He treats the life-saving abortion operation in the same way, holding that there is no direct choice against life involved in chopping up the foetus if what is intended as end is to save the life of the mother and what is intended as means is no more than the removal of the foetus and the consequential relief to the mother's body.[36] As a suasive, he points again to the fact that *if* an artificial womb or restorative operation were available for the aborted foetus, a right-thinking mother and doctor in such a case would wish to make these available to the foetus; this shows, he says, that a right-thinking mother and doctor, even where such facilities are *not* in fact available, need not be regarded as intending the death of the foetus they kill.[37] For my part, I think Grisez's reliance on such counter-factual hypotheses to specify the morally relevant meaning or intention of human acts is excessive, for it removes morally relevant "intention" too far from common-sense intention, tends to unravel the traditional and common-sense moral judgments on suicide (someone would say: "It's not death I'm choosing, only a long space of peace and quiet, after which I'd willingly be revived, if that were possible"!), and likewise disturbs our judgments on murder and in particular on the difference between administering (death-hastening) drugs to relieve pain and administering drugs to relieve-pain-by-killing.

In any event, the version of traditional nonconsequentialist ethics which has gained explicit ecclesiastical approval in the Roman church

35. *Ibid.*, p. 333 and pp. 89-90 respectively.

36. *Ibid.*, p. 341 and p. 94 respectively.

37. *Ibid.*, p. 341 and p. 95 respectively. I agree with Grisez that the fact that, if an artificial womb were available, many women would *not* transfer their aborted offspring to it shows that those women are directly and wrongfully intending the *death* of their offspring. I suspect Judith Thomson would agree; cf. p. 22.

these last ninety years treats the matter differently; it treats a bad or
unwanted aspect or effect of act A_1 as an *intended* aspect of A_1, not
only when the good effect (unlike the bad) follows only by virtue of
another human act A_2, but also *sometimes* when both the good effect
and the bad effect are parts of one natural causal process requiring
no further human act to achieve its effect. *Sometimes*, but not always;
so when?

A variety of factors are appealed to explicitly or relied on implicitly
in making a judgment that the bad effect is to count as intended-as-a-
means; Bennett would call the set of factors a "jumble";[38] but they are
even more various than he has noted. It will be convenient to set them
out while at the same time observing their bearing on the two cases
centrally in dispute, the craniotomy to save a mother's life and that
notable scenario in which "you reach around to your back and unplug
yourself from that violinist to save your life."

(1) Would the chosen action have been chosen if the victim had
not been present? If it would, this is ground for saying that the bad
aspects of the action, viz. its death-dealing effects on the victim
(child or violinist), are not being intended or chosen either as end
or means, but are genuinely incidental side effects that do not necessarily determine the character of one's action as (not) respectful of
human life. This was the principal reason the ecclesiastical moralists
had for regarding as permissible the operation to remove the cancerous womb of the pregnant woman.[39] And the "bitter" reaction which
Foot cites and endorses—"If you are permitted to bring about the death
of the child, what does it matter how it is done?"—seems, here, to miss
the point. For what is in question, here, is not a mere matter of tech-
nique, of different ways of doing something. Rather it is a matter
of the very reason one has for acting in the way one does, and such
reasons can be constitutive of the act as an intentional performance.

38. Jonathan Bennett, " 'Whatever the Consequences,' " *Analysis* 26 (1966):
p. 92 n. 1.
39. See the debate between A. Gemelli and P. Vermeersch, summarized in
Ephemerides Theologicae Lovaniensis 11 (1934): 525-561; see also Noonan,
The Morality of Abortion, p. 49; Zalba, *Theologiae Moralis Compendium* I,
p. 885.

One has no reason even to want to be rid of the foetus within the womb, let alone to want to kill it; and so one's act, though certain, causally, to kill, is not, intentionally, a choice against life.

But of course, *this* factor does not serve to distinguish a craniotomy from unplugging that violinist; in both situations, the oppressive presence of the victim is what makes one minded to do the act in question.

(2) Is the person making the choice the one whose life is threatened by the presence of the victim? Thomson rightly sees that this is a relevant question, and Thomas Aquinas makes it the pivot of his discussion of self-defensive killing (the discussion from which the "doctrine" of double effect, as a theoretically elaborated way of analyzing intention, can be said to have arisen). He says:

Although it is not permissible to intend to kill someone else in order to defend oneself (since it is not right to do the act "killing a human being," except [in some cases of unjust aggression] by public authority and for the general welfare), still it is not morally necessary to omit to do what is strictly appropriate to securing one's own life simply in order to avoid killing another, for to make provision for one's own life is more strictly one's moral concern than to make provision for the life of another persons.[40]

As Thomson has suggested, a bystander, confronted with a situation in which one innocent person's presence is endangering the life of another innocent person, is in a different position; to choose to intervene, in order to kill one person to save the other, involves a choice to make himself a master of life and death, a judge of who lives and who dies; and (we may say) this context of his choice prevents him from saying, reasonably, what the man defending himself can say: "I am not choosing to kill; I am just doing what—as a single act and not simply by virtue of remote consequences or of someone's else's subsequent act—is strictly needful to protect my own life, by force-

40. *Summa Theologiae* II-II, q.64, art. 7: "Nec est necessarium ad salutem ut homo actum moderatae tutelae praetermittat ad evitandum occisionem alterius: quia plus tenetur homo vitae suae providere quam vitae alienae. Sed quia occidere hominem non licet nisi publica auctoritate propter bonum commune, ut ex supra dictis patet [art. 3], illicitum est quod homo intendat occidere hominem ut seipsum defendat."

fully removing what is threatening it." Now the traditional condemnation of abortion[41] concerns the bystander's situation: a bystander
cannot but be choosing to kill if (a) he rips open the mother, in a way
foreseeably fatal to her, in order to save the child from the threatening enveloping presence of the mother (say, because the placenta
has come adrift and the viable child is trapped and doomed unless it
can be rescued, or because the mother's blood is poisoning the child,
in a situation in which the bystander would prefer to save the child,
either because he wants to save it from eternal damnation, or because
the child is of royal blood and the mother low born, or because the
mother is in any case sick, or old, or useless, or "has had her turn,"
while the child has a whole rich life before it); or if (b) he cuts up or
drowns the child in order to save the mother from the child's threatening presence. "Things being as they are, there isn't much a woman
can safely do to abort herself," as Thomson says (p. 8)—at least, not
without the help of bystanders, who by helping (directly) would be
making the same choice as if they did it themselves. But the unplugging of the violinist is done by the very person defending herself.
Thomson admits (p. 8) that this gives quite a different flavor to the
situation, but she thinks that the difference is not decisive, since bystanders have a decisive reason to intervene in favor of the *mother*
threatened by her child's presence. And she finds this reason in the
fact that the mother *owns* her body, just as the person plugged in to
the violinist owns his own kidneys and is entitled to their unencum-
bered use (p. 9). Well, this too has always been accounted a factor
in these problems, as we can see by turning to the following question.

(3) Does the chosen action involve not merely a denial of aid and
succor to someone but an actual intervention that amounts to an assault on the body of that person? Bennett wanted to deny all relevance
to any such question,[42] but Foot[43] and Thomson have rightly seen that
in the ticklish matter of respecting human life in the persons of others,
and of characterizing choices with a view to assessing their respect for
life, it *can* matter that one is directly injuring and not merely failing

41. *Ibid.*, arts. 2 and 3.
42. Bennett, " 'Whatever the Consequences.' "
43. Foot, "The Problem of Abortion and the Doctrine of Double Effect," pp.
11-13.

to maintain a life-preserving level of assistance to another. Sometimes, as here, it is the causal structure of one's activity that involves one willy-nilly in a choice for or against a basic value. The connection between one's activity and the destruction of life may be so close and direct that intentions and considerations which would give a different dominant character to mere nonpreservation of life are incapable of affecting the dominant character of a straightforward taking of life. This surely is the reason why Thomson goes about and about to represent a choice to have an abortion as a choice *not* to provide assistance or facilities, *not* to be a Good or at any rate a Splendid Samaritan; and why, too, she carefully describes the violinist affair so as to minimize the degree of intervention against the violinist's body, and to maximize the analogy with simply refusing an invitation to volunteer one's kidneys for his welfare (like Henry Fonda's declining to cross America to save Judith Thomson's life). "If anything in the world is true, it is that you do not commit murder, you do not do what is impermissible, if you reach around to your back and unplug yourself from that violinist to save your life" (p. 8). Quite so. It might nevertheless be useful to test one's moral reactions a little further: suppose, not simply that "unplugging" required a *bystander's* intervention, but also that (for medical reasons, poison in the bloodstream, shock, etc.) unplugging could not safely be performed unless and until the violinist had first been dead for six hours and had moreover been killed outright, say by drowning or decapitation (though not necessarily while conscious). Could one then be *so* confident, as a bystander, that it was right to kill the violinist in order to save the philosopher? But I put forward this revised version principally to illustrate *another* reason for thinking that, within the traditional casuistry, the violinist-unplugging in Thomson's version is *not* the "direct killing" which she claims it is, and which she *must* claim it is if she is to make out her case for rejecting the traditional principle about direct killing.

Let us now look back to the traditional rule about abortion. If the mother needs medical treatment to save her life, she gets it, subject to one proviso, even if the treatment is certain to kill the unborn child—for after all, her body is *her* body, as "women have said again and again" (and they have been heard by the traditional casuists!). And the proviso? That the medical treatment not be *via* a straightforward assault on or intervention against the child's body. For after all *the child's body is the child's body, not the woman's.* The traditional casuists have admitted the claims made on behalf of one "body" up to the very limit where those claims become *mere (understandable) bias, mere (understandable) self-interested* refusal to listen to the *very same* claim ("This body is *my* body") when it is made by or on behalf of another person.[44] Of course, a traditional casuist would display an utter want of feeling if he didn't most profoundly sympathize with women in the desperate circumstances under discussion. But it is vexing to find a philosophical Judith Thomson, in a cool hour, unable to see when an argument cuts both ways, and unaware that the casuists have seen the point before her and have, unlike her, allowed the argument to cut both ways impartially. The child, like his mother, has a "just prior claim to his own body," and abortion involves laying hands on, manipulating, that body. And here we have perhaps the decisive reason why abortion cannot be assimilated to the range of Samaritan problems and why Thomson's location of it within that range is a mere (ingenious) novelty.

(4) But is the action action against someone who had a duty not to be doing what he is doing, or not to be present where he is present? There seems no doubt that the "innocence" of the victim whose life is taken makes a difference to the characterizing of an action as open to and respectful of the good of human life, and as an intentional killing. Just how and why it makes a difference is difficult to unravel; I shall not attempt an unraveling here. We all, for whatever reason, recognize the difference and Thomson has expressly allowed its relevance (p. 8).

But her way of speaking of "rights" has a final unfortunate effect at this point. We can grant, and have granted, that the unborn child has no Hohfeldian *claim-right* to be allowed to stay within the mother's body under all circumstances; the mother is not under a strict duty to allow it to stay under all circumstances. In *that* sense, the child "has no right to be there." But Thomson discusses also the case of the burglar

44. Not, of course, that they have used Thomson's curious talk of "owning" one's own body with its distracting and legalistic connotations and its dualistic reduction of subjects of justice to objects.

in the house; and he, too, has "no right to be there," even when she opens the window! But beware of the equivocation! The burglar not merely has no claim-right to be allowed to enter or stay; he also has a strict duty *not* to enter or stay, i.e. he has no Hohfeldian *liberty*— and it is *this* that is uppermost in our minds when we think that he "has no right to be there": it is actually unjust for him to be there. Similarly with Jones who takes Smith's coat, leaving Smith freezing (p. 9). And similarly with the violinist. He and his agents had a strict duty not to make the hook-up to Judith Thomson or her gentle reader. Of course, the violinist himself may have been unconscious and so not himself at fault; but the whole affair is a gross injustice to the person whose kidneys are made free with, and the injustice to that person is not measured simply by the degree of moral fault of one of the parties to the injustice. Our whole view of the violinist's situation is colored by this burglarious and persisting wrongfulness of his presence plugged into his victim.

But can any of this reasonably be said or thought of the unborn child? True, the child had no *claim-right* to be allowed to come into being within the mother. But it was not in breach of any *duty* in coming into being nor in remaining present within the mother; Thomson gives no arguments at all in favor of the view that the child is in breach of duty in being present (though her counter examples show that she is often tacitly assuming this). (Indeed, if we are going to use the wretched analogy of owning houses, I fail to see why the unborn child should not with justice say of the body around it: "That is my house. No one *granted* me property rights in it, but equally no one *granted* my mother any property rights in it." The fact is that both persons *share* in the use of this body, both by the same sort of title, viz., that this is the way they happened to come into being. But it would be better to drop this ill-fitting talk of "ownership" and "property rights" altogether.) So though the unborn child "had no right to be there" (in the sense that it never had a claim-right to be allowed to *begin* to be there), in another straightforward and more important sense it *did* "have a right to be there" (in the sense that it was not in breach of duty in being or continuing to be there). All this is, I think, clear and clearly different from the violinist's case. Perhaps forcible rape is a special case; but even then it seems fanciful to say that the child is or could be in any way at fault, as the violinist is at fault or would be but for the adventitious circumstance that he was unconscious at the time.

Still, I don't want to be dogmatic about the justice or injustice, innocence or fault, involved in a rape conception. (I have already remarked that the impermissibility of abortion in any such case, where the mother's life is not in danger, does not depend necessarily on showing that the act is a choice directly to kill.) It is enough that I have shown how in three admittedly important respects the violinist case differs from the therapeutic abortion performed to save the life of the mother. As presented by Thomson, the violinist's case involves (i) no bystander, (ii) no intervention against or assault upon the body of the violinist, and (iii) an indisputable injustice to the agent in question. Each of these three factors is absent from the abortion cases in dispute. Each has been treated as relevant by the traditional casuists whose condemnations Thomson was seeking to contest when she plugged us into the violinist.

When all is said and done, however, I haven't rigorously answered my own question. When should one say that the expected bad effect or aspect of an act is not intended even as a means and hence does not determine the moral character of the act as a choice not to respect one of the basic human values? I have done no more than list some factors. I have not discussed how one decides which combinations of these factors suffice to answer the question one way rather than the other. I have not discussed the man on the plank, or the man off the plank; or the woman who leaves her baby behind as she flees from the lion, or the other woman who feeds *her* baby to the lion in order to make good her own escape; or the "innocent" child who threatens to shoot a man dead, or the man who shoots that child to save himself;[45] or the starving explorer who kills himself to provide food for his fellows, or the other explorer who wanders away from the party so as not to hold them up or diminish their rations. The cases are many, various, instructive. Too generalized or rule-governed an application of the notion of "double effect" would offend against the Aristotelean, common law, Wittgensteinian wisdom that here "we do

45. This case is (too casually) used in Brody, "Thomson on Abortion," *Philosophy & Public Affairs* 1, no. 3 (Spring 1972): 335.

not know how to draw the boundaries of the concept"—of intention, of respect for the good of life, and of action as distinct from consequences—"except for a special purpose."[46] But I think that those whom Aristotle bluntly calls wise can come to clear judgments on most of the abortion problems, judgments that will not coincide with Thomson's.

IV

I have been assuming that the unborn child is, from conception, a person and hence is not to be discriminated against on account of age, appearance or other such factors insofar as such factors are reasonably considered irrelevant where respect for basic human values is in question. Thomson argues against this assumption, but not, as I think, well. She thinks (like Wertheimer,[47] mutatis mutandis) that the argument in favor of treating a newly conceived child as a person is merely a "slippery slope" argument (p. 3), rather like (I suppose) saying that one should call all men bearded because there is no line one can confidently draw between beard and clean shavenness. More precisely, she thinks that a newly conceived child is like an acorn, which after all is not an oak! It is discouraging to see her relying so heavily and uncritically on this hoary muddle. An acorn can remain for years in a stable state, simply but completely an acorn. Plant it and from it will sprout an oak sapling, a new, dynamic biological system that has nothing much in common with an acorn save that it came from an acorn and is capable of generating new acorns. Suppose an acorn is formed in September 1971, picked up on 1 February 1972, and stored under good conditions for three years, then planted in January 1975; it sprouts on 1 March 1975 and fifty years later is a fully mature oak tree. Now suppose I ask: When did that oak begin to grow? Will anyone say September 1971 or February 1972? Will anyone look for the date on which it was first noticed in the garden? Surely not. If we know it sprouted from the acorn on 1 March 1975, that is enough (though a biologist could be a trifle more exact about "sprouting"); that is when *the oak* began. *A fortiori* with the conception of a child, which is no *mere* germination of a seed.

46. Cf. Wittgenstein, *Philosophical Investigations* (Oxford, 1953), sec. 69.
47. Pp. 23-51.

Two sex cells, each with only twenty-three chromosomes, unite and more or less immediately fuse to become a new cell with forty-six chromosomes providing a unique genetic constitution (not the father's, not the mother's, and not a mere juxtaposition of the parents') which thenceforth throughout its life, however long, will substantially determine the new individual's makeup.[48] This new cell is the first stage in a dynamic integrated system that has nothing much in common with the individual male and female sex cells, save that it sprang from a pair of them and will in time produce new sets of them. To say that *this* is when a person's life began is not to work backwards from maturity, sophistically asking at each point "How can one draw the line *here*?" Rather it is to point to a perfectly clear-cut beginning to which each one of us can look back and in looking back see how, in a vividly intelligible sense, "in my beginning is my end." Judith Thomson thinks she began to "acquire human characteristics" "by the tenth week" (when fingers, toes, etc. became visible). I cannot think why she overlooks the most radically and distinctively human characteristic of all—the fact that she was conceived of human parents. And then there is Henry Fonda. From the time of his conception, though not before, one could say, looking at his unique personal genetic constitution, not only that "by the tenth week" Henry Fonda would have fingers, but also that in his fortieth year he would have a cool hand. That is why there seems no rhyme or reason in waiting "ten weeks" until his fingers and so on actually become visible before declaring that he *now* has the human rights which Judith Thomson rightly but incompletely recognizes.

48. See Grisez, *Abortion: The Myth, the Realities and the Arguments*, chap. 1 and pp. 273-287, with literature there cited.

Rights and Deaths

In the preceding article, John Finnis makes a great many adverse remarks about my article on abortion.[1] I cannot take them all up: there are too many. I shall instead concentrate on certain of his positive proposals. One of them (I take it up in section II) would, if true, make abortion impermissible in cases in which I think it permissible; and another (I take it up in section III) would, if true, undercut an argument I had used to support the permissibility of abortion in those cases, and in others as well. Both proposals have consequences well beyond the abortion issue, and so on any view call for close attention.

I

But first, some things Finnis says about rights. I *think* his main complaint against me in the part of his paper which deals with rights is that I was wrong to discuss them at all—my doing so "needlessly complicates and confuses the issue." I find this puzzling. My aim was to raise doubts about the argument that abortion is impermissible because the fetus is a person, and all persons have a right to life; and how is one to do that without attending to rights? But this is merely by the way. More interesting, I think, is this: I had said that the right to life was not unproblematic—that a man's having a right to life does not guarantee either that he has a right to be given the use of whatever he needs for life, or that he has a right to continued use of whatever he is currently using, and needs for life. So, I said, the right to life

1. Pp. 3-22.

will not serve the opponents of abortion in the very simple and clear way in which they seem to have thought it would. Finnis thinks my point about the right to life is correct and familiar enough: he has an explanation of it. He says that he will call, for example, one man's right to slit another's throat a "Hohfeldian right"; presumably one man's right to hit another on the nose is also a Hohfeldian right. Hohfeldian rights have the same "logical structure," he says: "to assert a Hohfeldian right is to assert a three-term relation between two persons and the action of one of those persons insofar as that action concerns the other person." So (I suppose) to assert:

(1) Alfred has a right to hit Bill on the nose,

is to assert that a three-term relation holds between Alfred, Bill, and a certain action. By contrast, to assert:

(2) Charles has a right to life,

is to assert that a two-term relation holds between Charles and a certain thing ("or state of affairs"). Rights such as are attributed by assertions of (2) "cannot be completely analyzed in terms of some unique combination of Hohfeldian rights"—i.e. (if I have understood this), sentences such as (2) are not analyzable into any function of sentences such as (1). And (he says) this fact is, though I did not recognize it, the explanation of what I drew attention to in the right to life.

Now I am inclined to think that this account of what one asserts when one asserts (1) and (2) has no future. Finnis has simply not noticed the difficulties which lie in wait for it.[2] What precisely is supposed to be the third term in the case of (1)? An actual, particular action of Alfred's, viz., his hitting of Bill on the nose? But what if there never is any such action, since Alfred never exercises his right? Or perhaps, instead, the third term is an act-kind? But if so, which? And what precisely is supposed to be the second term in the case of (2)? Life? Charles's continuing to live? And what if his continuing to

2. Actually, a rather dark footnote (10) suggests that Finnis may not really mean what he said. For in the footnote it appears that "inadequate specification" of the action someone had a right to have done for him may make for trouble. Whereas if a relation holds amongst three things, it holds amongst them however they are specified.

live does not exist, since he does not continue to live, since he gets killed? The mind reels.

I suspect that what lurks behind Finnis's account is a grammatical difference: in (1), the phrase "right to" is followed by a verb phrase, and indeed a verb phrase whose main verb ("hit") is what some philosophers call an "action verb." By contrast, in (2), the phrase "right to" is followed by a noun phrase ("life"). And perhaps his point, then, is this: that sentences like (2) in this respect are not analyzable into sentences like (1) in this respect. ("He has a right to life" is presumably equivalent to "He has a right to live"; but I suppose it would be said that the verb "live" is not an "action verb.") If this is his point, he may for all I know be right—we should need to be told how to recognize an "action verb" when we meet one, but perhaps Finnis could tell us this.

But for present purposes, it doesn't matter whether he can or not, or even whether this is his point or not: for his aim was to explain what I drew attention to in the right to life, and *that* is not explainable by *any* difference between the logic or grammar of (2) on the one hand, and sentences such as (1) on the other.

For the fact is, I was simply over-fascinated by the example currently on the table. I said that a man's having a right to life does not guarantee either that he has a right to be given the use of whatever he needs for life, or that he has a right to continued use of whatever he is currently using, and needs for life. The right to life is a natural right; and being fascinated by the right to life, I noticed only that analogous points hold of all the natural rights. I should have noticed that analogous points hold of *all* rights. If Alfred very much wants to hit Bill on the nose, Bill might well sell him the right to do so—Bill sells, Alfred buys, and then has the right. Does he have a right to be given the use of whatever it is he needs if he is to hit Bill on the nose? If Bill has been carried off by an eagle, and can only be reached by helicopter, does Alfred have a right to be given a helicopter? Hardly. If Alfred steals your helicopter, and is on his way to Bill, does he have a right to continued use of your helicopter? Scarcely.

The situation about rights, it seems to me, is really this: *all* of them are problematic in the way I mentioned—none of them will serve anybody in the very simple and clear way in which opponents of abortion have seemed to think the right to life would serve them. Unlike Mr. Finnis, I think there does not exist any even remotely plausible theory of the logic of rights. And yet, again unlike Mr. Finnis, I think there does not exist any issue of importance in ethics in which we can avoid or side-step them.

II

I had suggested in my article that it is morally permissible for you to unplug the ailing violinist from yourself to save your life, even though to unplug him is to kill him. "Quite so," says Finnis. I had then asked: so why not abortion in analogous circumstances? What if a woman is pregnant due to rape, and allowing the child to remain inside her endangers her life? May she not arrange for an abortion to save her life? Finnis replies: (1) That would be *direct* killing of the innocent, and direct killing of the innocent is always impermissible. (2) Your unplugging the violinist from yourself to save your life is only *indirect* killing. Indirect killing is not always permissible, but it sometimes is—in particular, indirectly killing that violinist is.

A very important difference, then, this difference between direct and indirect killing: it bears a heavy moral weight. And I am not convinced that Finnis has made clear how it is able to carry that weight.

He puts it like this. Your killing of someone is direct if your choice in acting is "a choice against life"; and he says—anyway, I *think* he means to say[3]—that a choice is a choice against life where it is a choice to bring about a death, either as an end in itself, or as a means to some further end. You directly kill a person if your choice in acting is a choice to bring about a death, either as end or means. By contrast, you only indirectly kill a person if, though you foresee his death will be a consequence of what you do, your choice in acting is not a choice to bring about his death, either as end or means. (I had said in a footnote in my article that what matters is whether or not the *killing* is

3. Because on p. 103 he asks himself: "When *should* one say that the expected bad effect or aspect of an action is not intended either as end or as means and hence does not determine the moral character of the act as a choice not to respect one of the basic human values?" I take it that if an expected bad effect, say a death, is *not* intended as end or as means, then the act which causes the death does not issue from a choice against life, and hence the agent does not directly kill.

the agent's end or means; Finnis says that what matters is whether or not the *death* is the agent's end or means. There are reasons to prefer my account, but I am content to adopt his in what follows.)

Two questions present themselves: (1) Why should it be thought that this difference makes a moral difference? (2) If it makes a moral difference, does it make the moral difference Finnis wants it to?

The difficulties to which question (2) points are familiar enough, and I shall not spend much time over them.[4] I suppose Finnis is right to say that if you unplug the violinist, you only indirectly kill him: since you unplug him to save your life, his death is not your end (your end is the saving of your life), and it is not your means either (your means to the saving of your life is the unplugging you do). But what if a woman is pregnant due to rape, and allowing the child to remain inside her endangers her life? Suppose she takes a medicine known to cause miscarriage,[5] and takes it in order to cause miscarriage in order to save her life? The child's death is not her end (her end is the saving of her life), and it is not her means either (her means to the saving of her life is the medicine she takes and the miscarriage it causes). So here too the killing should be indirect. But if it is indirect, it should be permissible, for just as you unplug the violinist to save your life, she takes the medicine to save her life. Yet on Finnis's view *she* acts wrongly, she does the impermissible.

Finnis needs to have the woman's killing of the child turn out to be direct killing, and your killing of the violinist to be indirect killing. And I am afraid he has not succeeded in getting what he needs. He mentions four questions we should ask about a putative indirect killing. (a) "Would the chosen action have been chosen if the victim had not been present?" If so, there is reason to say the killing is in-

4. See, for example, Philippa Foot, "The Problem of Abortion and the Doctrine of the Double Effect," *The Oxford Review* 5 (1967), and Thomas Nagel, "War and Massacre," *Philosophy & Public Affairs* 1, no. 2 (Winter 1972). I should at this place mention how much I have learned about the matters dealt with in this section, not merely from these two articles, but from the discussions of them at the Society for Ethical and Legal Philosophy.

5. I had not known there were such medicines. But Finnis tells us that if a pregnant woman's life is threatened by fever, it is permissible for her to take or be given a medicine to reduce the fever, even though it is known that the medicine causes miscarriage. (In *this* case, then, the killing must be indirect.) So perhaps there are.

direct: the death is not the agent's end, but is a mere (foreseen) side effect of the action he takes to reach his end. But as Finnis himself grants, *this* will not distinguish between the cases we are looking at: "in both situations, the oppressive presence of the victim is what makes one minded to do the act in question." (b) "Is the person making the choice the one whose life is threatened by the presence of the victim?" Yes, in both cases. (c) "Does the chosen action involve not merely a denial of aid and succor to someone but an actual intervention that amounts to an assault on the body of that person?" No more in the one case than in the other. What Finnis has in mind in raising this question is that we should contrast with your unplugging the violinist, not a woman's neatly and cleanly taking a teaspoon of medicine, but rather a craniotomy, i.e. an operation in which the child's skull is crushed to make it possible to get it out of its mother. (And a craniotomy, of course, the mother is not likely to be limber enough to perform herself.) You can unplug the violinist, thereby killing him, while wearing white gloves; in a craniotomy you have actually to take hold, and it is far too messy for that. But I cannot think that Finnis means us to take this point very seriously. Abortifacients one could take by teaspoon would then be morally safe, and the existing procedure for a late abortion (the use of a saline solution) only slightly less so. Jonathan Bennett poured scorn on this kind of consideration in the article which Finnis cites, and I think he was quite right to do so. (d) "But is the action against someone who had a duty not to be doing what he is doing, or not to be present where he is present?" I think Finnis supposes there is more fault in the case of you and the violinist than in the case of the woman and child: in the former case, "the whole affair is a gross injustice." I should have thought there was no need to remind anyone of the injustice in rape. But more important, it is hard to see how anyone could think that this question has any bearing at all on the question whether a given death is, on the one hand, an agent's end or means, or on the other hand, a mere foreseen consequence of what he does to save his life.

Still, it might be said that perhaps the killing in the case of woman and child (but not in the case of you and the violinist) really is a direct killing, even though Finnis has just not argued very well for it. Or again, it might be said (Professor Grisez, for example, would say) that the killings in both cases are indirect, and Finnis has simply been wrong in thinking that while one is permissible, the other is not. So it seems to me that we should turn back to question (1), and ask—Mr. Finnis, his arguments, his moral views apart—why it should be thought that this difference which we are now looking at makes a moral difference.

Some people may think that Finnis has already sufficiently answered this question when he asked us to notice that a direct killing involves a choice "against life." Isn't that bad? And isn't it plain that a man's choices, intentions, reasons have a bearing on the moral evaluation proper to what he does?

Of course they do. But a man who kills only indirectly foresees perfectly clearly that he will bring about a death, and chooses the act he knows will bring it about. What we need to know is why it should matter so crucially whether the death a man foresees is, on the one hand, his end or means, or on the other hand, a merely foreseen consequence.

Sometimes what is done for us is just this: we are given sample acts in which a death is a man's end or means. Here a man kills for nothing further, he kills merely out of hate; there a man kills for money. And the acts are indeed horrendous. Alongside these are set acts in which though a man kills, and the death he brings about is foreseen, it is neither his end nor his means. Here is a bombardier, assigned the task of destroying a missile site which has been launching a rain of deadly missiles onto his country. Unfortunately there is a child on the site, the sick two-year-old daughter of the missile site's commanding officer. If the bombardier drops his bombs, that child will be killed. Most regrettable that the thing has to be done, yet plainly not a horrendous act if he goes ahead.

But this enterprise, fascinating though it may be, proves nothing at all. A man may perform a dreadful deed while wearing boots, and a permitted, even a quite good deed, while barefoot. This hardly establishes the (hitherto unnoticed) moral significance of boots.

What is needed is to show that the difference *makes* the moral difference, or at least contributes to it. And the best way to test such a claim is to isolate the difference so far as possible. We should try to get as clear a direct killing and as clear an indirect killing as we can,

which so far as possible differ only in that respect, and then look to
see if a moral difference emerges.

Imagine the following:

(3) A violent aggressor nation has threatened us with death unless we allow ourselves to be enslaved by it. It has, ready and waiting, a monster missile launcher, which it will use on us unless we
surrender.

So far, so good. Nothing bizarre yet. Unfortunately, while I think the
missile launcher it has trained on us is perfectly possible, it is not such
as the average violent aggressor nation has as yet aspired to.

(3) (continued): The missile launcher has interior tunnels, each
leading to a missile. For technical reasons, the tunnels had to be
very small; for technical reasons also, each missile has to be triggered by a human hand. Midgets are too large. So it was necessary
to train a team of very young children, two-year-olds in fact, to
crawl through and trigger the missiles.

There are two possible continuations of this story. We might imagine
two worlds, in both of which (3) is true, but in one of which (4) is,
and in the other of which (5) is:

(4) Their technology being what it is, they were able to build
only one missile launcher; it will take at least two years to produce
another. (By contrast, training the team of children was easy, indeed, was done in a day.) We are capable of bombing the site. Unfortunately, if we bomb to destroy the launcher to save our lives, we
kill the children.

(5) Their psychology being what it is, they were able to train
only one team of children; it will take at least two years to train
another. (By contrast, building the launcher was easy, indeed, was
done in a day.) We are capable of bombing the site. Unfortunately,
bombing the site will save our lives only if by bombing we kill the
children.

Now I take it that if (4) is true, and we act, we only indirectly kill the
children: their deaths are not our end, nor do we need their deaths
if we are to achieve our end—our end would be just as well achieved

if by some miracle the children survive the bombing. Cases such as this have standardly been regarded as cases of indirect killing in the literature on this topic. By contrast, if (5) is true, and we act, we directly kill the children: their deaths are necessary to the achieving of our end, and if, by a miracle, they survive the bombing, we must bomb again.

Of course some very high-minded people may say we must not bomb in either case: after all, the children are innocent! Lower-minded people, like me, will say we can bomb in either case: after all, it is the violent aggressor nation which itself imposed that risk on the children. But what I think no one can say is that we may bomb if (4) is true, but not if (5) is. If that were true, a violent aggressor nation would do well to aspire to such a missile launcher. Careful engineering of tasks and supplies so as to insure the truth of (5) would guarantee it could swallow the virtuous at leisure.

I suspect that the most likely response to what I have said is: those children are not really innocent in the sense intended in the principle "Direct killing of the innocent is always impermissible." "Innocent" here does not mean "free of guilt," but has a technical sense:[6] perhaps "not currently doing harm, or about to do harm in the immediate future," perhaps "not part of the threat directed at others." The children on the launching team are no doubt free of guilt (they mean no one any harm), but they are part of the threat to us, for they are precisely the ones who will launch the missiles against us.

But how is this supposed to bear on the issue at hand? Finnis seemed to think that the innocence or lack of innocence of the victim has a bearing on the question whether he is killed directly or indirectly—see his question (d) above. But then were we misled as to the difference between direct and indirect killing? We were told it was a matter of whether the victim's death is end or means, or merely a foreseen consequence; and how could the victim's innocence, in the technical, or perhaps in any other, sense bear on *that*? After all, the children are not innocent in the technical sense in either (4) or (5); yet the one killing is indirect, the other direct.

I did indeed take a liberty when I said, above, that cases such as our act in (4) have standardly been regarded as cases of indirect killing in

6. Thomas Nagel, *op. cit.*, draws attention to this.

the literature on this topic. What we have standardly been offered are cases in which the victims are innocent in this technical sense. (Compare the sick daughter of the missile site's commanding officer in the case of the bombardier, cited above.) Whereas the children in (4) are not innocent in the technical sense. Nevertheless it was appropriate to take that liberty, for our act in (4) is exactly like the cases we have standardly been offered in those respects which define "indirect killing." It is unlike them in other respects—which only makes clear that the cases we have been offered did not isolate the difference whose moral significance they were intended to convince us of.

In the absence of a new account of the difference between direct and indirect killing, I suspect that innocence is best seen as having a bearing, not on whether a killing is direct or indirect, but rather on whether or not a given direct killing is permissible. Anyone who accepts this is then in a position to explain why the act in (5) is permitted, just as the act in (4) is: though the act in (5) is, unlike the act in (4), a direct killing, still its victims are not innocent in the technical sense, and it is only direct killing *of the innocent* in the technical sense which is categorically ruled out.

But on the other hand, to accept this is also to grant that the difference between direct and indirect killing does not have the moral significance which has been claimed for it. The acts in both (4) and (5) are both permitted, though one is a direct, the other an indirect killing.

And to accept it is also to open the door for abortions in cases in which the child itself is part of the threat to the mother, and hence is not in the technical sense innocent. Such abortions no longer fall under the categorical ban, it having been only a play on the word "innocent" which made it seem that they did fall under it.

III

Finnis rightly says that it was my intention to assimilate certain cases in which a woman allows a pregnancy to continue to cases in which a man is a Good Samaritan to another; and similarly, to assimilate her refusing to allow the pregnancy to continue, to cases in which a man refuses to be a Good Samaritan to another. My further intention was to draw attention to the fact that there are circumstances in which it is morally acceptable for a man—and so similarly, for the woman—to refuse, to say "No, the cost is too great, and I will not pay it."

Finnis believes he has a crushing proof I was wrong to do this. "And here," he says, "we have perhaps the decisive reason why abortion cannot be assimilated to the range of Samaritan problems and why Thomson's location of it within that range is a mere (ingenious) novelty." So we should look where he points.

What we find is this: "The child, like his mother,[7] has a 'just prior claim to his own body,' and abortion involves laying hand on, manipulating, that body." I *think* his point is this. A man who refuses to be a Good Samaritan, lays hands on no one, he manipulates no one, he does harm to no one; he merely refrains from giving aid. By contrast, the woman who aborts herself (if she can) does lay hands on and manipulate the child. Well, perhaps she does not actually *touch* it. But she certainly does it a harm: she kills it, in fact. So the decisive reason why I am wrong in making the assimilation is this: a reluctant Samaritan merely does not save a life, whereas the mother actually kills the child.

Now it had not actually escaped my notice that the mother who aborts herself kills the child, whereas a man who refuses to be a Good Samaritan—on the traditional understanding of Good Samaritanism—merely does not save. My suggestion was that from a moral point of view these cases should be assimilated: the woman who allows the pregnancy to continue, at great cost to herself, is entitled to praise in the same amount, and, more important, of the same kind, as is the man who sets forth, at great cost to himself, to give aid. That is why I proposed we attend to the case of you and the violinist: surely if you allow the violinist to remain plugged into you, at great cost to yourself, you deserve praise in the same amount, and of the same kind, as any traditional Good Samaritan—and how does this differ from the case of

7. Here I feel the waters rising. Finnis had said in a footnote that a right to decide what happens in and to one's body is "to be equated, apparently" with a just prior claim to one's own body; so here he is saying that both child and mother have a right to decide what happens in and to their bodies. Earlier, however, he had said, with éclat, that "traditional Western ethics simply does not accept that a person has 'a right to decide what shall happen in and to his body.' " Has traditional Western ethics changed its mind? and so quickly?

woman and child? To say "Ah, but if she refuses, she kills, whereas a man who refuses to set forth to give aid merely refrains from saving" is not only not decisive against my assimilation, it is *no* reason at all to think it improper—in the absence of a showing that (a) the difference between killing and not saving makes a moral difference, and indeed that (b) the difference between killing and not saving makes a sufficiently profound moral difference as to make the assimilation improper, and of course also that (c) the truth of (b) does not conflict with its being permissible for you to refuse to sustain the violinist, i.e. with its being permissible for you to unplug him, thereby killing him.[8]

Finnis has not only not produced these showings, he seems not to have seen they are needed. This *may* be because he thinks that not saving is the same as indirect killing, and therefore already shown to differ morally from real (read: direct) killing. Why else, after all, would he have advised us that if we want to know whether an agent kills directly or indirectly, we should ask whether he makes an assault, or merely denies aid? (Compare question [c] of the preceding section.) But it is, simply, a *mistake* to think that not saving is indirect killing. An indirect killing is perforce a killing, whereas it is quite possible that a man has never killed, and yet that there are many lives he did not save.

Or, alternatively, it *may* be because he thinks (a), (b), and (c) so obvious as to need no argument. My own view is that none of them is obvious. It seems to me to be an interesting, and open, question whether or not (a) is true, and I want to make a few brief suggestions about it below. However (b) strikes me as false, and in fact as shown to be false by the story of you and the violinist; so as is plain, I think (c) false too. As I cannot see that any reasons have been advanced to think (b) true, I shall from here on ignore it, and therefore (c) as well.

8. Finnis must show (c) as well as (a) and (b), since he agrees with me that you may unplug the violinist. It *may* be that Baruch Brody ("Thomson on Abortion," *Philosophy & Public Affairs* 1, no. 3 [Spring 1972]) does not have to show (c) as well as (a) and (b). Brody puts forward the same ground for rejecting the assimilation as Finnis does, but unlike Finnis, does not say you may unplug the violinist. On the other hand, he does not explicitly say you may not. All he explicitly says on the matter is that my "account of the violinist" is "very problematic."

Is (a) true? Once again it is noteworthy that the sample acts offered to convince us of the moral significance of the difference do not isolate it.[9] Here is a man who commits a gross and bloody murder; horrendous, isn't it? There is a man who is asleep, and therefore is not saving lives; scarcely horrendous, surely permissible for a man to sleep! But of course there are other things at work here besides the fact that one kills and the other does not save. For one thing, the sleeper does not know he is not saving, whereas the murderer knows he kills. So let us instead compare:

(6) David is walking across a field. Unbeknownst to him, a sick baby has burrowed its way under a clump of hay ahead of him. He steps on the clump, thereby killing it.

(7) Edward is walking across a field. Unbeknownst to him, a sick baby has burrowed its way under a clump of hay alongside his path. He walks on; the baby dies; he did not save it.

Is there a moral difference here? This brings me to the first point I wished to make about (a): its defenders will have to make a decision. Do they wish to say that although neither David nor Edward is at fault or to blame for what they do, or for what happens, still their acts differ morally? Or do they wish to say that the acts do not differ morally, that the important difference is not between killing and not saving, but between knowingly killing and knowingly not saving?

I propose we side-step this, and restrict ourselves to cases in which both men act knowingly. A second difference between committing murder, and not saving while asleep, is that the murderer aims at a death whereas the sleeper does not, and this too contributes to the moral difference between them. So let us instead compare:

(8) Frank hates his wife and wants her dead. He puts cleaning fluid in her coffee, thereby killing her.

(9) George hates his wife and wants her dead. She puts cleaning fluid in her coffee (being muddled, thinking it's cream). George

9. Michael Tooley, pp. 52-80, also draws attention to this, and tries to isolate the difference in order to show it is not morally significant.

happens to have the antidote to cleaning fluid, but he does not give it to her; he does not save her life, and she dies.

Horrendous, both!—but if (a) is true, what Frank did should be worse than what George did, and is it? I suspect that if anyone feels that it is, this is because he thinks of Frank as having done *two* morally significant things: first he imposed a risk on his wife by poisoning her coffee, and then, like George, he did not save her. (Maybe he did not have an antidote, but surely he could have called for an ambulance.) So he and George both did not save; but Frank had imposed the risk because of which his wife needed saving, and it is plainly bad to impose risks on people even if no harm actually comes to them. I suspect that it may, ultimately, be this[10] which inclines people to opt for (a). But should we? What if there were no room at all for saving once the agent had made his move?

Whatever we think about Frank and George, it does seem to be very difficult to construct a clear and convincing pair of cases in which the difference is isolated (knowledge, intentions, and reasons are so far as possible the same), but in which the one who kills acts badly, and the one who refrains from saving does not. I suppose that (a) could be true, even if this could not be done; but it does cast doubt on it.

What does seem plain is just this: the question of (a)'s truth is so far an open one. It needs attention of a kind which Mr. Finnis has certainly not paid it, and in the absence of which his objection to the assimilation I made is merely so much hand waving.

10. And the connected point that a man who wants not to save, and did not impose the risk, can always ask that fascinating question "Why me?"

THE CONTRIBUTORS

JOHN FINNIS is a Fellow and
Praelector in Jurisprudence, University
College, Oxford, and Reader in
Commonwealth and American Law
in the University of Oxford. Articles
of his have appeared in legal and
philosophical books and journals in the
United States, England, and Australia.
He is now at work on a book on natural
law and natural rights.

JUDITH JARVIS THOMSON is Professor
of Philosophy at Massachusetts
Institute of Technology. Her articles—
primarily on issues in ethics and the
philosophy of mind—have appeared in
philosophical journals here and abroad.

MICHAEL TOOLEY is Assistant Professor
of Philosophy at Stanford University.

ROGER WERTHEIMER has taught
philosophy at Portland State, the
University of Oregon, and the Graduate
Center of the City University of New
York. He is the author of *The
Significance of Sense* and holds a
Guggenheim Fellowship for the
academic year 1973-1974.

A *Philosophy & Public Affairs* Reader

Titles available:

EQUALITY AND PREFERENTIAL TREATMENT
MARX, JUSTICE, AND HISTORY
MEDICINE AND MORAL PHILOSOPHY

THE RIGHTS AND WRONGS OF ABORTION
WAR AND MORAL RESPONSIBILITY